The Art of Fugue

The Art of Fugue

BACH FUGUES FOR KEYBOARD, 1715–1750

Joseph Kerman

Includes a CD with New Recordings
by Davitt Moroney and Karen Rosenak

UNIVERSITY OF CALIFORNIA PRESS
Berkeley   Los Angeles   London

University of California Press
Berkeley and Los Angeles, California

University of California Press, Ltd.
London, England

Library of Congress Cataloging-in-Publication Data

Kerman, Joseph, 1924–
    The art of fugue : Bach fugues for keyboard, 1715–1750 / Joseph Kerman.
      p.   cm.
    Includes bibliographical references (p.   ) and index.
    Includes compact disc.
    ISBN 0-520-24358-7 (cloth : alk. paper)
    1. Fugue.   2. Bach, Johann Sebastian, 1685–1750. Keyboard music.   I. Title.
    MT59.K49   2005
    786'.1872'092—dc22

2005004045

Recording engineer for the CD: Robert Schumaker. Tracks 1–2 and 7–8 were recorded at International House, University of California, Berkeley, on February 8, 2004; track 3 at the same location on February 23, 2004; track 4 at Chapel of St. Joseph of Arimathea, Berkeley, on April 28, 2004; and tracks 5–6 at Hertz Hall, University of California, Berkeley, on January 24, 2004. Tracks 16 and 17 are from *Die Kunst der Fuge, BWV 1080,* ed. Davitt Moroney (Munich: G. Henle Verlag, 1989), reproduced by permission of G. Henle Verlag.

Manufactured in the United States of America

14   13   12   11   10   09   08   07   06   05
10 9 8 7 6 5 4 3 2 1

To
Ellen Rosand,
thirty-year friend

A song that is well and artificially made cannot be well perceived nor understood at the first hearing, but the oftener you shall hear it, the better cause of liking you will discover.

William Byrd

What I can offer has a meaning only for those who have heard, and who keep on hearing. To such I may be able to give a suggestion here and there for renewed hearing.

Søren Kierkegaard

Contents

Contents of the CD   *xi*

Preface   *xv*

Acknowledgments   *xxi*

1   Fugue in C Major: *The Well-Tempered Clavier*, book 1   *1*

2   Fugue in C Minor: *The Well-Tempered Clavier*, book 1   *11*

3   Fughetta in C Major, BWV 952   *17*

4   Fugue in C-sharp Minor: *The Well-Tempered Clavier*, book 1   *23*

5   Contrapunctus 1: *The Art of Fugue*   *33*

6   Contrapunctus 10: *The Art of Fugue*   *39*

7   Chromatic Fantasy and Fugue, BWV 903   *51*

8   Prelude and Fugue in E-flat Major:
The Well-Tempered Clavier, book 1   *65*

9   Fugue in E Major: *The Well-Tempered Clavier*, book 2   *75*

10   Fugue on "Jesus Christus unser Heiland": *Clavierübung*,
book 3   *85*

11   Fugue in F-sharp Minor: *The Well-Tempered Clavier*, book 1   *95*

12   Gigue: English Suite no. 3 in G Minor   *103*

13   Fugue in A-flat Major: *The Well-Tempered Clavier*, book 1   *109*

14   Fugue in A Minor: Fantasy and Fugue in A Minor,
BWV 904   *115*

15   Fugue in B-flat Major: *The Well-Tempered Clavier*, book 2   *125*

16   Fugue in B Major: *The Well-Tempered Clavier*, book 2   *133*

Afterword   143
Notes   149
Notes to the CD   155
Glossary   159
Bibliography   167
Index   171

Contents of the CD

Recording information is given on the copyright page.
Details about the instruments and musical sources
may be found on page 157.

RECORDINGS (TRACKS [1]–[8])

[1]–[2]   Prelude and Fugue in C Major:
The Well-Tempered Clavier, book 1
Karen Rosenak, *piano*   1:27 / 1:52

[3]   Fughetta in C Major, BWV 952
Davitt Moroney, *clavichord*   1:54

[4]   Fugue on "Jesus Christus unser Heiland":
Clavierübung, book 3
Davitt Moroney, *organ*   4:52

[5]–[6]   Fantasy and Fugue in A Minor, BWV 904
Davitt Moroney, *harpsichord*   2:46 / 5:34

[7]–[8]   Prelude and Fugue in B Major:
The Well-Tempered Clavier, book 2
Karen Rosenak, *piano*   1:43 / 3:28

9 – 10 Prelude and Fugue in C Major:
The Well-Tempered Clavier, book 1

11 – 12 Prelude and Fugue in C Minor:
The Well-Tempered Clavier, book 1

13 Fughetta in C Major, BWV 952

14 – 15 Prelude and Fugue in C-sharp Minor:
The Well-Tempered Clavier, book 1

16 Contrapunctus 1: *The Art of Fugue*

17 Contrapunctus 10: *The Art of Fugue*

18–19 Chromatic Fantasy and Fugue, BWV 903

20–21 Prelude and Fugue in E-flat Major:
The Well-Tempered Clavier, book 1

22–23 Prelude and Fugue in E Major:
The Well-Tempered Clavier, book 2

24 Fugue on "Jesus Christus unser Heiland":
Clavierübung, book 3

25–26 Prelude and Fugue in F-sharp Minor:
The Well-Tempered Clavier, book 1

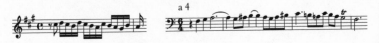

27   Gigue: English Suite no. 3 in G Minor

28–**29**   Prelude and Fugue in A-flat Major:
The Well-Tempered Clavier, book 1

30–**31**   Fantasy and Fugue in A Minor, BWV 904

32–**33**   Prelude and Fugue in B-flat Major:
The Well-Tempered Clavier, book 2

34–**35**   Prelude and Fugue in B Major:
The Well-Tempered Clavier, book 2

Preface

This is a book of commentaries on selected Bach fugues—
"essays in musical analysis and appreciation," one might call
them, to enlarge on the title of Donald Francis Tovey's famous
Essays in Musical Analysis. The fugues are keyboard fugues, written for clavichord, harpsichord, and organ. About half of them
come from the two books of *The Well-Tempered Clavier (WTC),*
the other half from a variety of other sources, some of them less
familiar: Bach's comprehensive keyboard publication *Clavierübung* (Keyboard Practice), *Die Kunst der Fuge* (The Art of
Fugue), the English Suites, and other manuscript sources. The
music stems from all periods of Bach's career except for the ear-
liest. The Chromatic Fantasy dates most probably from his
Weimar years, around 1715, and the two contrapuncti from *The
Art of Fugue* reached their definitive form when Bach revised the
work just before his death in 1750.

Annotations of any extent on Bach fugues are hard to find
outside of the technical literature, and I have taken the time to do

justice, as best I can, to these short but very rich pieces. The discussion is geared to individual segments and bars within the fugues, so readers will need the sheet music with the bars numbered. Most of those who come to this book will already own copies of the *WTC,* the source of many of the pieces, and some of the other selections too. The CD enclosed with this book makes it possible to view or print out all the scores, those you lack and those you may like to have in an extra copy.

Also on the disc are performances of five of the fugues discussed below, specially recorded for this book by Davitt Moroney and Karen Rosenak.

One inspiration for the present work was Tovey, whose lapidary and marvelous annotations to his edition of the *Well-Tempered Clavier* are classics. First published in 1924, they were reprinted in 1994 to accompany an authoritative new musical text of the *WTC,* prepared by Richard Jones. As a publication of the Associated Board of the Royal Schools of Music, Tovey's contribution was appropriately didactic; his annotations read like a piano teacher's docket of instructions about touch, fingering, ornaments, and so on, for every place that needs them. But his instructions always rest on his *understanding* of the music, and what he has to say about that makes, or should make, his commentaries required reading for anyone interested in the fugues, not only students. My purpose is critical, not didactic. I write about reading and listening to fugues, not performing them— listening to them and understanding them.

Another inspiration for me was not a text but a musical anthology, *Bach: The Fugue,* an elegant collection of nine fugues, some with preludes, edited by Charles Rosen for the Oxford

Keyboard Classics in 1975. We have not a few items in common.
There are profound words in Rosen's introduction:

> The "pure" fugue, the meditative fugue, is basically a key-
> board work for Bach. Of course the fugal texture can be
> adapted to many forms: the dance, the concerto, the aria,
> the chorale-prelude. But the fugue *tout court* . . . is almost
> without exception conceived for keyboard in the early
> eighteenth century. Only the performer at the keyboard
> is in a position to appreciate the movement of the voices,
> their blending and their separation, their interaction and
> their contrasts. A fugue of Bach can be fully understood
> only by the one who plays it, not only heard but felt through
> the muscles and nerves. Part of the essential conception of
> the fugue is the way in which voices that the fingers can feel
> to be individual and distinct are heard as part of an insepa-
> rable harmony. The confusion of vertical and horizontal
> movement is one of the delights of fugue.

And again:

> The keyboard fugue, for Bach, is essentially private. . . .
> The proper instrument is what one has at home: harpsi-
> chord, clavichord, organ or piano. There are few of these
> fugues that exploit the resources of any particular instru-
> ment; many would go equally well with sonorities as
> different as organ and clavichord.

What I have in my home is a piano, and I expect most readers of
this book will be pianists too. The music on the CD is played on
all of these instruments.

The fugues that I have selected are, to me, also select; the commentaries attempt to convey something of what makes them
particularly beautiful, powerful, intriguing, witty, or moving.

This can only be done, I believe, by following the music closely, seeing, hearing, and Rosen would say *feeling* how the melodic lines are shaped and combined, how the harmonies unfold, and how time spans are articulated. My hope is to reach the broadest range of musicians: not only performing artists—harpsichordists and pianists—students, and musicologists, but also amateur players: home pianists who have often found themselves drawn to Bach over the years, often to pieces they have known for as long as they can remember, and whose deep pleasure in them is not blunted too much by cautious tempos, uneven articulation, or even a certain amount of stumbling. This community is said to be dead or dying, but I reckon the reports are exaggerated.

The technical level of my discussions will not be high enough for some professionals. I hope it will not seem unduly high to amateurs. At a few points where the discussion gets detailed I format the text in smaller type with bullets. It is not possible to deal properly with fugue without employing technical language—a language in which anyone who has had music lessons is already a beginning speaker. We know words for pitch and rhythm, chord and key, if not for stretto and inversion (yet). A glossary has been carefully compiled to explain technical concepts and exemplify them, by means of page references in the text and bar numbers in the scores on the CD. For intrepid readers the glossary can serve as a self-tutor.

The commentaries are independent and can be read separately. The first two can also be read as a pair laying out the basic facts of fugue.

No commentary is provided on the preludes that introduce many of the fugues discussed below, or the fantasy from the Fantasy and Fugue in A Minor. Fugue is the topic here; the

Prelude in E-flat Major from the *WTC,* book 1, is discussed only because it includes, exceptionally, a fugue (an exceptional fugue). This lacuna will seem to some a dereliction, even an outrage, and no doubt a more methodical author would have made it his business to "cover" the preludes. Or a less self-indulgent one; having written several books about entire repertories before, this time I only wanted to write about music that engages me wholly, and that I feel I can write about effectively. I chose my fugues. Bach chose the preludes.

But scores for the preludes and the A-Minor Fantasia are available on the CD, like the fugues, so one can see them, study them, and play them together with their fugues. Some can also be heard on the CD (tracks 1, 5, and 7).

NOTE

Clarifying marks are used when melodic lines and progressions are indicated by letters in the text:

directional arrows ↗ and ↘ for larger leaps
the stroke | for barlines
the mark ∫ for sequences

Acknowledgments

I acknowledge without irony the sympathetic if inconclusive consideration given to earlier versions of this book by several publishers; as the process took some time, I was able to rethink and fine-tune the thing considerably. And I am of course most appreciative to Mary Francis, Rose Vekony, and Lynne Withey of the University of California Press for carrying publication through so splendidly. The recordings were supported by the O'Neill Fund at the University of California at Berkeley, and I am both grateful and delighted that my colleagues Davitt Moroney and Karen Rosenak agreed to make them. Robert Schumaker was the expert and very patient recording engineer.

Michael Markham not only checked the text, filled out footnotes, and so on, but also engaged in a dialogue about it. In effect he was another insightful reader, along with the knowing press referees. The text owes a great deal to the comments of friends, some of whom mulled over early draft chapters—Charles Fisk and Davitt Moroney in particular, O. W. Neighbour, Ellen

Rosand, and the late David Lewin, a consummate, gentle musician, composer, and profound thinker about music. Peter Kerman is the amateur home pianist I refer to in the foreword.

I am very grateful to all of them, and also to David Ledbetter for sending me his book on *The Well-Tempered Clavier* in typescript before publication, an act of courtesy from which I greatly benefited. Thanks also to Christopher Hatch for a remark in a review some years ago which, though he can have no idea, helped me understand my own project. The essay on the Fugue in C-sharp Minor from the *WTC,* book 1, appeared in *Eighteenth-Century Music* 1 (2004): 79–84.

The routine in my earlier books was to keep the formal acknowledgments sincere, short, and simple; but as would be the case for many veteran musicians, I am sure, sustained engagement with the Bach fugues has taken on characteristics of a *Künsterleben* for this one, and the occasion seems to require something more. My indebtedness goes all the way back to the petite Russian lady who gave me the Fughetta in C Major and the two-part Fughetta in C Minor, the music master whose idea of a sight-reading test was the Fugue in D Minor from the *Well-Tempered Clavier,* book 1 (a bear), and the girl at summer camp who practiced F-sharp Minor in book 1 between rehearsals for *Too Many Girls.* At Princeton Professor Oliver Strunk explained the evolution of A-flat Major in book 2 and undergraduate Charles Rosen lectured me on G-sharp Minor. Carl Weinrich, one of America's first early music mavens, introduced me to the organ toccatas.

Not many in academia can have had so many inspired Bach players as actual colleagues, all of them inspirational to me. Even Carl can be counted as a colleague, since briefly I was his assistant organist at Princeton; then Warren Martin at Westminster Choir

College, Lawrence Moe at Berkeley, followed by Alan Curtis, John Butt, Davitt Moroney, and for one semester Ralph Kirkpatrick, who inaugurated the Ernest Bloch Visiting Professorship at the University of California at Berkeley in 1962 with a *Well-Tempered* marathon, not only playing the whole forty-eight in public twice, on harpsichord and clavichord, but also giving master classes and public lectures and even team-teaching (with me) an undergraduate course on it.

C Minor in book 2 was a bone of contention . . . after concerts Ralph would unwind at a steak house in Oakland, with Alan and me in attendance, patiently nursing our beers. Much later, after both Alan and John Butt had left Berkeley, John unknowingly triggered the present book with a gift of his CD of the Bach Toccatas and Fugues and the "Schübler" Chorales for Harmonia Mundi. The excitement of rediscovering the "Dorian" Prelude and Fugue in his performance spilled over to other fugues. Suddenly, mysteriously, I found myself writing.

Music consoles, in a way I did not really know before spending the last couple of years with Bach, at a difficult period. *Du holde Kunst, ich danke dir dafür.* I thank Johann Sebastian Bach— to me an austere, remote, but incontestably benign figure, like others in my life: William Byrd, Oliver Strunk, and first of all my father, the writer William Zukerman. His support extended all the way down to buying me a Smith-Corona when I was a boy and then searching out venues for my teenage music criticism, though he had no ear for music. It was my mother who loved music, sang beautifully, and smiled when she sang.

Joseph Kerman
Berkeley, April 3, 2004

CHAPTER I

Fugue in C Major

The Well-Tempered Clavier, Book 1

The Well-Tempered Clavier is an exemplary collection of twice twenty-four preludes and fugues for keyboard in which Bach exhibits his unsurpassed contrapuntal virtuosity and also the seemingly infinite types, forms, and characters that may emerge—at his hands, and at his hands alone—from the art of fugue.

> Some pieces are sketches for jeweled miniatures, some for vast frescos. Some are intimate and lyrical; some quiver with the intensity of passion that is equally intensely controlled; some fringe on the pedantic; and some are frankly sublime. Part of their fascination resides in the many possible attitudes from which they can be viewed, and in the manifold aspects they can assume. What seemed schematic may reveal new freshness; what seemed dull emerges as merely misunderstood; what seemed limited displays new dimensions; to what by its very richness and concentration has become indigestible, we return after days, months, or even years, to receive new and unanticipated nourishment and revelation. One may occasionally lay aside the *WTC,* but never because of its exhaustibility.

These are words by Ralph Kirkpatrick, the leading harpsi-
chordist, after Landowska, of the mid-twentieth century, who
recorded the *WTC* twice and wrote a book about it. Few musicians have engaged with this music more deeply.

A particularly exemplary function is usually adduced for the
pair of concise fugues at the head of book 1 of the *WTC*. The
Fugue in C Major, preceded by a famous and also exemplary
prelude, displays maximum learning: a stretto fugue fitting two
dozen entries of a one-and-a-half-bar subject into little more
than two dozen bars of music. Strettos come at many different
time and pitch intervals.

The importance that Bach attached to stretto is evident from
The Art of Fugue, another exemplary work, which requires a
whole series of stretto fugues to exemplify this most widely used
of the so-called fugal devices. Stretto is formed when one voice
carrying the fugue subject is "answered" by the subject in
another voice before the first voice has finished. It heightens the
subject in a complicated way—or, rather, in one of many complicated ways; the effect can be peremptory, intense, majestic, or
serene. The Fugue in C Major uses an array of strettos to build
intensity, to unsettle a fundamental rhythmic pattern, to generate modulations, and to prepare a registral climax. Another
stretto brings the composition to rest.

Not even the stretto fugues of *The Art of Fugue* are as single-
minded as the Fugue in C Major, whose twenty-seven bars
include no episodes and, apart from subject entries, no more
than a total of two bars of transitional music preparing the
fugue's three cadences . . . plus a miniature peroration in which
the whole thing gently goes up in smoke, up to a high C we have

never heard before. The three cadences—structural cadences—terminate and define the fugue's large sections, or phases, as it sometimes seems better to call them. The word "section" suggests something carved out in space, as with a pizza, and while "phase" is not a term usually employed by music theorists for a unit of time, the dictionary definition is suggestive: "a stage in a process of change or development."

To work many different strettos on a relatively long subject, such as this one, must also be considered an achievement. Fourteen notes is long for a subject designed for multiple strettos. The typical stretto-fugue subject runs to about half that length (six notes in the Fugue in E Major from the *WTC,* book 2, for example: see page 75).

The number fourteen carried special resonance for this composer, being the total of numbers derived from his name: 2 (B) + 1 (A) + 3 (C) + 8 (H). He chose a number to sign the beginning of the *WTC,* just as later he would personalize the end of *The Art of Fugue* with a theme: B♭ (in German terminology, B) A C B♮ (H). He also chose to open his exemplary collection of twenty-four preludes and fugues with a fugue that brings its subject twenty-four times.

Then the next fugue in the collection has no strettos or other artifice at all, beyond contrapuntal inversion at the octave. The Fugue in C Minor is a very *knowing* fugue but it is not a *learned* fugue; it flaunts minimal learning. As Hermann Keller writes in his book on the *WTC,* it "owes its extraordinary popularity with players as much to the charm of its subject as to its easy comprehensibility and transparent polyphony. . . . This fugue is in everything the complete antithesis of the first one"—as we will hope to see on pages 11–15.

First Phase: *Bars 1–13*

In spite of the technical prowess that one might suppose this fugue was meant to demonstrate, as the flagship fugue of *The Well-Tempered Clavier,* more than one commentator has exclaimed over its natural, spontaneous quality and quiet eloquence. Certainly the piece wears its learning lightly. What it really demonstrates is that learning and eloquence are not mutually exclusive: a fundamental lesson. Bach, "the deepest savant of contrapuntal arts (and even artifice), knew how to subordinate art to beauty," a leading literary journal declared in 1788. (The anonymous writer was almost certainly Carl Philipp Emanuel Bach.)

Fugues start up slowly and methodically. After one voice alone announces the fugue subject in the opening exposition— here it is the alto voice—the others enter one after another, enriching the texture from a single melodic line to two-part polyphony, three-part polyphony, and so on. Bach omits the short links usually found between some of the later voice-entries of an exposition ("merely interstitial episodes," Tovey calls them), serving notice that this is to be a very compressed fugue. Since the subject extends over a bar and a half, its four appearances establish a definite hypermeter of three half notes' duration.

Donald Tovey, though now a distant figure, will be cited again and again in this book. Though the center of his universe was Beethoven, as I have written elsewhere, Tovey did some of his most penetrating scholarly-critical work in reference to Bach.

The continuation of the original subject in a fugue, called the countersubject, probably deserves that name only when it is maintained as a functional feature later in the composition, along with the subject. The fluent continuation material here does not quite reach that status; yet it plays an elegant role in the fugue's exposition and conclusion. The sixteenth-note sequential figure of bars 2–3 (A G F E ∫ F E D C ∫ D C B | A) emerges from the subject's opening figure as a diminution and is itself treated to melodic inversion. Basic tools of Bach's workshop, sequence, diminution, and inversion can be applied almost unobtrusively, as here, but also more pointedly for a variety of expressive effects.

The Fugue in C Major, a four-voiced fugue, brings the subject successively in the alto, soprano, tenor, and bass and then goes on at once to a fifth entry in the soprano with a close stretto entry on its heels (saturation!). This stretto is a strict canon in the tenor at the time interval of a quarter note and the pitch interval of an upper fifth; in one contrapuntal inversion or another—that is, with the second voice entering above or below the first, in any octave—this is the main stretto that Bach will make use of throughout the piece. The fifth entry itself *confirms* the macro-metrical pulse of three half notes, and if the stretto (the sixth entry) *breaches* it, the break seems calculated to allow the next entries to march all the more strongly in the modular slow triple meter. They modulate first to G and then to A minor.

The key of A minor, the submediant, is affirmed by the fugue's first strong cadence—though as often happens with structural articulations in Baroque music, the music starts up again at once in the tonic key C major without any modulatory process. Bach prepares this cadence as briefly as possible, or just about. It is interesting that he also wanted to make it as expressive as possible, as though to counteract the rather dry, abstract nature of the basic material. He did the same with the next cadence (in D minor).

Second Phase: *Bars 14–19*

In this small stretch of music much happens. Starting in C major with the "default" stretto we already know—it therefore sounds as though we are starting all over again—Bach lays down a barrage of further stretto entries at different time intervals and different scale degrees. Several entries are reinforced by doubling in thirds *[bars 15, 17, 19]*.

This classic pileup is one of the passages Laurence Dreyfus has in mind when he refers delicately in his book *Bach and the Patterns of Invention* to the "irritations" in Bach's voice leading—awkward sounds in certain of the canonic dispositions "that he attempted to eliminate, perhaps without achieving an unqualified success." But these attempts, by adding ingenious covering counterpoint in the noncanonic voices, contribute to some of the most expressive moments in the fugue, as Dreyfus points out.

He cites bars 17–19. The A-minor cadence in bar 14 had activated a run of subject entries all starting from the pitches C and G in one octave or another, but now they are topped by a tenor entry starting from A *[bars 17–18]*. The melodic line moves up to D and then to F, the tenor's highest note in the fugue so far. The upper voices also rise to the top of their ranges around now; the soprano, as usual, is the voice to watch, for the curling eighth-note scale that it traces invests the registral climax with special power and radiance. This scale merges two entries, one incomplete and the other complete *[bars 15–17]*, advancing from G above middle C up to the higher C and then to high F, A, and ultimately B♭, just one note short of the top of Bach's keyboard.

Example 1

The harmony tilts expansively to the subdominant, as the texture opens up in bars 16–17—where I always hear a spectral fifth
voice, according to the model in example 1. (It is not uncommon
for Bach to divide a fugue subject, clearly heard, between two
voices.) What I am hearing is the dazzling eruption of high
trumpets and drums in the Gratias of the B-Minor Mass, a fugue
with evident points of contact with the present *WTC* fugue.

Third Phase: *Bars 19–27*

The climactic high B♭ in the soprano echoes a moment later in a
bass entry pointed toward the next cadential goal, D minor *[bar
18]*. D minor balances the previous minor key, A minor. (The
large-scale tonal progression from here to the end of the fugue,
the circle of fifths A–D–G–C, will be articulated by pedals in the
bass.) But a "default" stretto at the upper fifth overlaps the actual
cadence and casts a strange filtered light over it. A novel effect,
this seems to arise from a compound of the unexpected D-major
harmony—with F♯—the pause on the pedal D, brief as it is, and
the way the two inner voices ease their way or glide across the
cadential downbeat. B♮ also rather pointedly contradicts the climactic B♭s heard earlier *[bar 19]*.

The progression conveys something of the mood of an interrupted, or deceptive, cadence, though technically it cannot be called that, of course, and to call the D-major chord a *tierce de Picardie* also seems odd, for Picardy mode-change is supposed to happen to the tonic chord at the end of a composition, not to the dominant of the dominant somewhere in the middle. At key points earlier in the fugue—after the exposition, and after the A-minor cadence—the function of the default stretto was to move the music forward. By this time it feels valedictory, almost nostalgic.

It initiates a beautifully calculated slowdown. After the stately momentum of the first phase of this fugue, and the whirl of virtuosic exertion in the second, the concluding phase brings a peaceful stretto that feels like a duplication, *stretto* without *sforzo,* without stress *[bars 20–24].* This stretto is drawn out at the lower sixth over a pedal G.

One more, final stretto comes above the third and longest pedal, a prolongation of the cadential note C *[bars 24–27].* Tinges of subdominant harmony relax the music further—how precisely the B♭s are positioned in bars 24–26—and relaxation also extends to the form of the subject. As a general rule, the statement of the subject that comes at or near the end of a fugue makes a definitive statement, sometimes aphoristic or witty, sometimes climactic or monumental. Not here. What we get here is a very informal and mild free entry in the soprano, which skips a few beats while restoring (with some help from the alto) its long-forgotten continuation, that sequential figure in sixteenth notes (A G F E ∫ F E D C). With which the soprano guides the melodic line back down to its opening note, the tonic, C *[bars 24–26].*

The music is coming to a close—heretofore the subject has ended less conclusively, on the third degree, not the tonic—and on C the subject converges with C in the pedal, two octaves below. Still, this turns out to be rather fragile as a place of rest, and the wispy upward scales at the end do not contribute much to stability. Perhaps they are Bach's way of nudging us to move right along to the next number, the antithetical Prelude and Fugue in C Minor.

Fugue in C Minor

The Well-Tempered Clavier, Book 1

Bach's very best-known fugue must be the Fugue in C Minor
from book 1 of *The Well-Tempered Clavier.* It has become standard teaching material in advanced and elementary textbooks
alike, for courses in canon and fugue as well as lowly Music
Appreciation. It was the first fugue to be jazzed and the first to
be switched on. Heinrich Schenker, lord and master of modern
music theory, settled on it as the example to expound in a classic
essay, "Organicism in Fugue," which recently provoked an entire
critical chapter from Laurence Dreyfus in his book *Bach and the
Patterns of Invention.* When *The New Grove Dictionary of Music
and Musicians* dropped Roger Bullivant's solid article "fugue"
from its second edition, what replaced it was (among other
things) a blow-by-blow analysis of the Fugue in C Minor.

There is a manuscript copied by one of Bach's students containing analytical annotations to this work. (Some are given by
David Schulenberg in *The Keyboard Music of J. S. Bach.*) "For the
use and improvement of musical youth eager to learn," reads

the title page for the *WTC;* did the Fugue in C Minor occupy a special place in the composer's personal curriculum?

One can even detect a mild backlash as regards the piece, as when Bullivant reaches the chapter on fugal form in *his* book on fugue and says he will look "not at the standard examples (*WTC* I C-Minor is the great favorite for an introduction to Bach's technique, *WTC* I C-Major being, for good reasons, beyond the understanding of the conventional theorist!) but at some of the more 'difficult' and, it is hoped, interesting forms." Assuming that Bach wanted to exhibit something minimal at (or very near) the beginning of his exemplary collection of preludes and fugues, C Minor indeed presented itself as a prime candidate.

Bullivant does not fail to note points of interest in this less-than-difficult composition, such as a "humorous fake entry" as early as bar 6 and the hidden entry of the subject at what sounds like the halfway mark of a sequential episode *[bar 11];* compare also bar 20.

One might add to these points Bach's astute choice of exactly the most incisive features of the subject from which to build the first episode, namely the downward leap of a sixth and the syncopation near the end of the subject. This episode returns later in another key and another contrapuntal inversion *[bars 5–6, 17–19];* a second episode also returns, in this case without inversion *[9–10, 22–23].* Recurring episodes are an attractive feature of this fugue and similar ones in the *WTC.*

Astute—and I think we could also call it ideally didactic. "Like *this,* like *this,* like *this,*" Bach is saying in the threefold sequence of bars 5–6. If Bach planned this early item in the *WTC* for teaching purposes, he must be suspected of the eighteenth-century equivalent of dumbing down . . . but then or now, this is a process that need by no means be unsophisticated. What is interesting is the way exaggerated simplicity coexists here with a whole array of skillful details.

For example, bars 13–14 may seem like a heavy-handed lesson in the treatment of scales in contrary motion. Yet the bland left-hand thirds are derived with a sort of exasperated wit from the near-continuous thirds just previously, themselves due to a revision in the second countersubject to make it work in the major mode (in the first half of bar 12, strict inversion would require eighth notes C B♭ A♭ B♭ in the alto).

Those countersubjects plod—as Bach must have wanted. And when Hermann Keller spoke of the music's "easy comprehensibility" he may have had in mind the unusually simple parade of two-bar phrases (subject, episode, subject, episode, and so on) at the start and throughout the first half of the composition. But once the later episodes become extended *[bars 17–19, 22–26],* the later entries sound freer and stronger. Another fine touch is the bold, energizing octave transposition of the second countersubject in bar 21.

Keller was right: it is the subject in this fugue that everyone finds *reizend,* charming, spirited, piquant, perky. Its gavotte-like rhythm permeates the whole piece. Only the "Little" G Minor Fugue for Organ has, for organists at least, a subject with the same sort of charisma. It is possible to feel that a tune like this should not be saddled with countersubjects that deflect attention. And it is not.

As the commentators all remark, the Fugue in C Minor demonstrates contrapuntal inversion very well, with five of the six possible permutations of the subject (s), countersubject 1 (cs 1), and countersubject 2 (cs 2) clearly on display:

bars	1–2	3–4	7–8	11–12	15–16	20–21	26–28	29–31
SOPRANO	—	s	cs 1	s	cs 1	s	cs 2	s
ALTO	s	cs 1	cs 2	cs 2	s	cs 1	cs 1	—
BASS	—	—	s	cs 1	cs 2	cs 2	s	(chords)

As this table illustrates, fugue gives composers a perfect way to show how a rich contrapuntal complex of subject and one or more countersubjects can be built up, step by step, from simple beginnings, and then to show off the same complex in many different lights. The subject sings out in the soprano or half-hides in the alto or supports the whole complex in the bass. The same basic harmonies will be heard over and over again, always with a slightly different nuance.

This fugue also teaches about the conventional closure of minor-mode music in the major, by altering the interval of a minor third in its final tonic chord into the more conclusive major third (the so-called *tierce de Picardie;* here C + E♮). Again, the lesson is unsubtle, with the Picardy third highlighted by its position (the top voice) and linear preparation (the scale fragment outlining a spiky diminished fourth, A♭ G F E♮).

It seems a little strange, in fact, that this decidedly didactic fugue, which is nearly the shortest in the whole of the *Well-Tempered Clavier,* should reach so lofty a conclusion—the rhetorical stop, the grandiose chordal statement of the subject *[bars 28, 29–31].* We may be inclined to hear these gestures as a response to improvisational flourishes at the end of the preceding Prelude in C Minor. Or something like self-parody may be involved here, I like to think, a wry glance at impressive organ voluntaries that

Bach had written in earlier years, such as the Passacaglia and Fugue in C Minor, works driven by the Baroque dialectic of extravagance and order, fantasy and craft. Typically, in these works, flamboyant preludes prepare the ground for sober fugues with brilliant virtuosic flourishes at the end.

Coming at the front of the book, the Fugue in C Minor serves as a model for a number of others with lively, dance-like subjects and prominent recurring episodes, but they all close in quite a different spirit, with an epigram derived wittily from some previous material. To be sure, these similar pieces are almost all in the major mode. Examples in book 1 are the Fugues in E-flat, E, F-sharp, and B-flat Major.

In many fugues it is necessary to change the subject slightly at its second appearance so as to smooth over the move from one tonality, the tonic, momentarily to another, the dominant. The tonal answer, as this is called, being a little different than the subject, it gives the composer an extra element to work with; one could say that in the Fugue in C Minor the fifth-leap G↘C of the answer *[bar 3]* adds a bit of steel to the fourth-leap C↘G of the subject and suggests a sequence with A↘D in the next bar. But this is just a detail; Bach uses the tonal answer only one more time. The technicalities of tonal answering loom too large in the analysis of fugues. Ebenezer Prout's great treatise on fugue of 1891 requires two whole pages for "Answer" in the index, the longest item by far. The art of fugue lies in a nexus of long-range continuity and rhetoric, well past the stage of local joinery.

CHAPTER 3

Fughetta in C Major,
BWV 952

This appears to be one of the fugues that did not make the cut for *The Well-Tempered Clavier* when Bach reviewed earlier materials, in the early 1720s, as a first step in planning his project. It is a slight piece, no doubt, but amusing and clever—though cleverness is not the same thing as sophistication, and there is a certain impudence about it that probably would have ruled it out in any case. Bach is certainly willing to embrace comedy as well as the grander modes of expression, but only high comedy finds its way into the *WTC*.

On the matter of sophistication: a fugue subject of any length in uninterrupted sixteenth notes was thoroughly old-fashioned by this time, though Bach had written many in youthful compositions. Example 2 shows the subjects of an early fugue in A minor and another fughetta that Bach copied into the *Clavier-büchlein für Wilhelm Friedemann Bach,* the little study book he began compiling for his oldest son in 1720. This fughetta is numbered 953 in the Schmieder catalog of Bach's works (BWV 953);

Example 2

a. Fugue in A Minor, BWV 944

b. Fughetta in C Major, BWV 953

our piece is BWV 952. The works are quite similar, and young piano students ever since have known them both from the collections of Little Preludes and Fugues issued by various publishers. These fughetta subjects can seem like throwbacks, especially that of BWV 953, a weaker piece all around.

Still, viewed differently, the brevity and a certain rhythmic quirk in the subject of BWV 952 hint at a spoof of those old-fashioned straggling subjects, for those in the know. On this view, the subject counts as the first of an almost breathless string of witticisms or antics coming up in this little composition. The rhythmic quirk arises from a slightly irregular accent thrown by an upbeat figure onto an *even* beat of the bar, beat 2 of the subject's first bar, in conjunction with regular accents on the *odd* beats, beat 3 of this bar and beats 1 and 3 of the next.

That upbeat figure, an *ascending* fourth filled in by sixteenth notes, is the key motivic element in BWV 952 (see example 3a). It functions in a lively passage of preparation for the strong cadence in bar 8. It returns with new piquancy at the second

Example 3

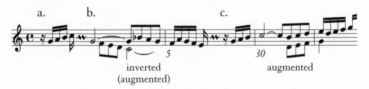

appearance of this passage at the end of the composition, as we will see.

One can even spot the figure as early as bars 3–6, in the slow countersubject, where it can be seen to be inverted and with its sixteenth notes augmented to eighths (see example 3b) . . . though with material as neutral and as impoverished as this, no one is likely to take such thematic derivations seriously (that is, as something with serious aesthetic consequence). In fact as the music proceeds, the eighth-note figure—a filled-in *descending* fourth—is mostly replaced by a different eighth-note figure also involving a fourth, this time *ascending* by a leap *[bars 9–11]*.

The following are points of interest in this fughetta:

- *Bars 1–5:* The exposition entries follow one another after three half notes, rather than two, giving the piece a sort of time-release acceleration effect when $\frac{2}{2}$ meter replaces the de facto $\frac{3}{2}$ meter later—as also happens in the first fugue of the *Well-Tempered Clavier* and many others. More unusual in this exposition is to see the eighth-note countersubject, introduced at the soprano entry, coolly divided between the two upper voices at the bass entry, presumably for reasons of register *[bars 4–5]*. This may be irregular, but it can hardly be said to weaken the composition in any way. Later, as has just been remarked, the stepwise eighth-note figure appears less often than the figure with the leap, which nearly develops into a new countersubject.

- *Bars 5–8:* A suspiciously glib sequence emerging from the exposition accelerates and hits the ground running for an early cadence in the dominant. This makes a strong articulation, and a "rhyming" passage occurs at the end of the fugue, providing the kind of neat, decisive wrap-up that usually enlivens dances and other pieces in binary form. Bach wrote a number of other fugues with this sort of binary articulation—two figure in this volume: A-flat Major from book 1 of the *WTC* and B-flat Major from book 2—as well as fugal gigues in many of his keyboard suites. BWV 952 is a lopsided example.

- *Bars 13–15:* A pair of entries after the central cadence has led us to D minor, where the fugue suddenly changes style. It is hard to think of a move quite like this in any other Bach fugue, at least in any short one. For just a few bars it mimics a rhapsodic keyboard improvisation, beginning over a pedal, A (introduced very smoothly, very professionally). The motivic chatter of the subject dies down for the first time. The harmonic rhythm, hitherto very regular, relaxes for a moment, to good effect.

- *Bars 23–26:* This fughetta sets no store by consistent episodes; after another two entries and another cadence, the style changes again. Normal fugal writing gives way to trio texture, consisting of two matching upper voices over a swiftly moving bass, and a momentary dip into the *style galant.*

  Half-plaintive, half-amused, this episode draws on motifs from the subject only at the end of each sequence leg, answered—as a sort of putdown, perhaps—in inversion. The naive turn to the subdominant is another fresh touch *[bar 26].*

- *Bars 26–34:* A final array of subject entries (soprano, tenor, bass) culminates in the rhyming phrase that suggests binary structure. The tonic cadence in bar 34 balances the dominant cadence in bar 8. Bach modified the phrase subtly (as well as transposing it) so as to strengthen the feeling of finality, something he also helped by bringing back the de facto $\frac{3}{2}$ meter of the fugue's beginning in bar 26 and keeping that meter to the end.

A charming touch comes in bars 30–31. The very last entry rattles away in the low bass register for the first time, more like a reproof than an answer to the tenor entry just before. The original slow figure of bars 3–6, with its *descending* stepwise eighth notes, inverts (not for the first time) to trace an *ascending* fourth. Then it doubles itself in sixths for emphasis and slips directly into the original upbeat motif—that same ascending fourth in sixteenths (see example 3c). Presto, the countersubject was an inverted augmentation after all.

CHAPTER 4

Fugue in C-sharp Minor

The Well-Tempered Clavier, Book 1

Among the special features of *Bachanalia: The Essential Listener's Guide to Bach's* Well-Tempered Clavier—a well-meaning effort, though badly misconceived, in my view—are the author Eric Lewin Altschuler's picks for the Top Ten Fugues, the Top Ten Subjects, the Superstar Four, and so on.

Well, among the Four Most Pithy Subjects (C-sharp Minor and A-flat Major in book 1, C-sharp Major and E Major in book 2), C-sharp Minor ranks as the Superstar—the shortest, the most constrained, and the most obsessive. The subject consists of only five notes, drawn from four consecutive pitches, and it holds to the tonic intently, setting down on C♯ twice and leaning on it by means of the slow cadential progression 2–1 (D♯–C♯). The fugue admits only two form-defining cadences, at bars 35 and 59 (halfway through), and following the latter the subject marches up to hammer away at C♯ as many as eight times. More than a fair share of these entries are placed as prominently as possible, in the soprano or the bass. Although two spectacular tonal shifts interrupt this tonic parade, the subject returns in the tonic after each of them with renewed force.

As a trajectory for a fugue this certainly seems remarkable, though it has not excited much comment in the literature—as remarkable for the quality of rootedness itself as for the apparent relation between the subject of this fugue and its form. Organic theories of music, which grew up along with the Bach revival of the nineteenth century and took sustenance from it, lingered long into the twentieth and probably still linger. Might not the basic matter of a fugue project itself, as though organically, into the form of the whole? The Fugue in C-sharp Minor would appear to say so. The tonic obsession of its first four bars is "composed out" over its last fifty. Of the secondary pitches in the subject, D♯ will accommodate a subject entry and E a stretto.

On another level, the subject's aggressively dissonant interval of a diminished fourth (B♯↗E) stimulates expressive minor-mode harmonies throughout, sonorities enriched to the point of luxuriance in the passages that employ all of the five voice parts.

Section 1: *Bars 1–35*

Section 1 of the Fugue in C-sharp Minor treats the principal subject alone, and section 2 combines it with two faster subjects or countersubjects. Starting with the bass, the initial exposition proceeds inexorably through successively higher and higher voices, and once the texture is filled out, new entries surge up in a second exposition, maintaining or even amplifying the grandeur of the first.

The first few entries sustain a traditional-sounding countersubject and set up a three-bar hypermeter, of some importance later in the piece. But almost at once the process of exposition starts to waver or transmute. The three-bar meter dissipates, as does the countersubject, while the abbreviation of the subject's opening whole note into a half note as early as the third entry eases the flow and at the same time softens its character. Small irregularities in the protocol (a relaxed stretto *[bar 14]*, entries in the subdominant *[12, 22]*) disrupt the steady order—the logic, as one usually says—of fugal exposition.

One can imagine Bach feeling this music out at the keyboard, improvising. He seems less interested in building from the subject at this point than in mulling over another figure, a scale figure in quarter notes salvaged from the aborted countersubject. "Nothing more is heard of this [countersubject]," says Tovey, "except a figure of descending crotchets which, developed by inversion in bars 17–18, fills up most of the texture . . . after which it gives rise to the second subject." The mood is less cumulative than ruminative.

What Tovey is describing is a variety of Schoenberg's "developing variation"; developing variation is superimposed on fugal exposition here and could really be said to supplant it when major-mode entries defang the dissonant, lowering diminished fourth that lies at the heart of it *[bars 29–35]*.

(One can track the developmental process bar by bar: after the quarter-note scale figure is initially developed by means of imitation *[bars 9–12, 13–16]*, it grows into longer and longer lines: first one that curls up through a sixth *[17–19]*, then one that sails and slips down more than an octave *[24–27]*. The developmental tools in bars 17–18 are sequence and inversion, in bars 25–27 diminution. From bar 17 on, the figure generally appears in an expanded form, encompassing a fourth rather than a third.

Finally—a tiny point, but God is in the details—the scale figure accumulates an anterior note on a downbeat *[bar 30]*, touching off the longest line of all, a broken scale moving through several voices over nearly two octaves, opening up into the sonorous cadence *[bars 30–35]*.)

How exquisitely the scale figure "gives rise to the second subject," by rising still further, in a new diminution *[bar 36]*. But from now on the fugue becomes less ruminative than relentless.

Section 2: *Bars 35–59*

The first strong (almost the very first) cadence arrives at the mediant, E—already forecast at the end of the first exposition—and is undercut; still another exposition in the tonic begins when E major is canceled and the mediant C-sharp minor returns. This standard Baroque ploy becomes functional in this composition, for the next cadence, in the submediant G-sharp minor, is undercut in the same way.

In this new exposition the original subject comes with another, fluid second subject above it that during the answer continues its own steady descent undisturbed in the soprano, rather than migrating to another voice, like a regular countersubject. The point was evidently to generate a long descending line in the treble, for a similar one occurs in bars 82–88. Sinking movement predominates in the later stages of this composition; the partly chromatic descent in bars 67–73 and 99–105 stays in the ear as one of its most impressive affective gestures.

Material is doled out gradually, the second subject entering in bar 35, the vigorous third subject in bar 49, and a kickoff figure (also vigorous) added to the second subject in bar 43. The new exposition starts at three-bar intervals, like the first one. It tilts heavily toward the subdominant but proceeds via another major-mode entry (bar 54, with a rather startling stretto between the alto and the soprano) to a cadence in the submediant, A major.

Bars 59–94

But now say good-bye to the major mode. Few if any traces of it can be found in the fifty-odd bars that remain to the piece, up to the hungrily awaited, gratifyingly drawn-out *tierce de Picardie* at the very end.

The cadence in A major balances the previous E-major cadence; this key too is undercut, and the sense of starting over again in the tonic is plainer now both because the subject stands out in the soprano and because it finally reinstates its long-lost opening whole note *[bar 59]*. It hangs on to this weighty— indeed, as it now sounds, momentous—leadoff for the rest of the piece, producing eight granitic subject entries. It reverts to half notes only as an extra contribution to excitement during the stretto of bars 94–98.

(One other reversion comes in a much-discussed subdominant entry—heard clearly enough, though divided between two voices—at bars 85–88. The fugue's unusual bias toward the subdominant, site of five subject entries as against three in the dominant, would have been calculated to balance the upcoming excursion to the "double dominant.")

After the cadence in bar 59, the startup in the tonic does not lead to modulation along well-worn paths, to mediants and sub-mediants, as happened after bar 35. We are brought to new and radical keys by shock tactics. Almost directly after asserting the subject in C-sharp minor, the soprano comes back to repeat it, intensified, a whole step higher, in D-sharp minor. (The minor supertonic is of course a remote or extreme key in Bach's system, seldom figuring as the site for a fugal entry, and when it does, the entry is approached via a close key, not juxtaposed with the tonic, as happens here.) As though in response to this anomaly, the supertonic entry recoils in a downdraft of chromaticism. Implicit in the subject from the start, chromaticism becomes explicit at the moment of harmonic extremity.

Redress occurs in the form of a mighty rumble on the tonic at the very bottom of Bach's keyboard *[bars 73–76]*. (The low B♯ at this place must have been the reason he chose the key of C-sharp minor for this subject. This entry is the first entry in the bass since back in section 1.) Or perhaps Bach acted as agent provocateur, promoting the tonal shock in order to rationalize his tonic obsession. For remarkably, and certainly obsessively, right after the low bass entry two others arrive on the tonic, with all three subjects circulating through the five voices—an orgy of triple counterpoint. A fourth (!) tonic entry seems desperate to break out of a rut—bars 92–93 feel like a heroic bid for freedom.

The impasse is broken by another tonal shock, a famous multiple stretto that starts by superimposing E minor upon C-sharp minor. This jolts as violently, and as anomalously, as the earlier one from C-sharp to D-sharp minor.

Bars 94–115

If thematic material (or the lack of it) is considered the main marker of musical form, the remainder of the piece would have to count as a third discrete section, for the second subject stops dead at this juncture and never comes back. Hermann Keller imagined a "bitter battle" between the two other subjects, "in which the first countersubject by its nature is not equipped to take part." Of course the busy eighth-note flow had to stop to allow the stretto to make its effect, and to clear space for an ending in five-part polyphony.

But if this is a three-part structure, it is a highly eccentric one. The music rushes headlong through the putative point of articulation: bar 94 lacks both the strong stop and the tonal shift of bar 35 (and bar 59), and I can only hear the activity that flares up there as an intense, concentrated digression from the parade of tonic subject entries starting at bar 73. Tonal movement up the circle of fifths—entries on E B F♯ C♯: just the right harmonic process to heighten excitement, like the reversion from the opening whole note to a half note in bar 95, as noted above—hastily restores the tonic.

Stretto became a major issue in the academic fugue that was developed in the conservatories of the nineteenth century and that probably still haunts pedagogy today. The densest of strettos was supposed to be saved till the end of the composition, where it would provide a weighty climax. The Fugue in C-sharp Minor seems to provide an example: four appearances of a four-bar subject are pressed into a space of seven bars at a point not far from the end, and there are even more stretto appearances of the third subject. The latter experiences an efflorescence from now on, though the first subject, as expanded by Bach, holds its own also.

In another respect, however, the stretto here provides no model for the *stretto maestrale*. This is not a climax of weight (such as does occur in a closer model for that device, at the end

Example 4

105

of the one other *Well-Tempered Clavier* fugue in five parts: the book I Fugue in B-flat Minor). One could speak of a climax of agitation in the Fugue in C-sharp Minor, but the climax of weight comes later. The stretto is more like a momentary paroxysm in which the first and third subjects fight furiously, according to Keller, until oil is poured on the waters by seventeen gorgeous, slow-flowing bars of minor-mode polyphony that bring the fugue to rest. This is by far the fugue's longest passage using the full five-part texture.

Note the three-bar hypermeter, again, defined by the start of the stretto and the tonic entries at bars 97 and 100. The latter is another entry divided between two voices. One can also construe a ninth tonic entry starting at bar 104; see example 4.

It is hard to get too upset with anyone passionate enough about *The Well-Tempered Clavier* to write a whole book about it. One winces, though, to find the Fugue in C-sharp Minor not in *Bachanalia*'s Top Ten, or even Top Forty Fugues, but in the limbo of Eric Altschuler's Long, Slow, and Not My Favorite Club.

For this music has been greatly, even extravagantly admired. Mozart arranged it (in D minor) for string quintet, with a lovely new prelude, and it haunted Beethoven when he wrote his

Quartet in C-sharp Minor, Opus 131 (another work with a sub-dominant bias). For Philipp Spitta, the first great Bach scholar, it was an artwork

> of such vast breadth and sublimity, of such stupendous—even overwhelming—harmonic power, that Bach himself has created but few to equal it. It is as though we were drifting rapidly over a wide ocean; wave rises over wave created with foam, as far as the eye can reach, and the brooding heavens bend solemnly over the mighty scene—the surging forces of nature and helpless, devoted humanity.

The prelude too has been equally and rightly admired. David Schulenberg surely speaks for the consensus when he calls the Prelude and Fugue in C-sharp Minor "one of the great masterpieces of *WTC* I."

The work might almost have been calculated to impress the nineteenth century, when terse, pregnant motives were the order of the day. The exceptionally short subject rather resembles the "Muss es sein?" motif in another Beethoven string quartet, Opus 135, and it is not so far from the "Fate" motif in *The Ring of the Niebelung.* Hugo Riemann described it darkly as "absorbed in itself, moving round itself, decidedly turned away from the world—brooding—Beethovenish." (Probably the greatest of nineteenth-century musicologists, Riemann published a 400-page analysis of the *WTC* in 1890.) Grim enough by itself—the diminished fourth B♯–E is astonishingly potent—the subject builds up a kind of Byronic intensity through its obsessive same-key repetitions. What Classically minded critics might frown upon as redundant impressed the Romantics as relentless, fate-driven; one thinks of the "Dies irae" in Liszt's *Totentanz,* for instance (actually, Bach has drawn on another timeworn melody—that of the well-known Advent chorale "Nun komm, der Heiden Heiland").

When this music is not haunted and driven it is violently disrupted, at bars 66 and 94. One does not associate dramatic gestures of this kind with Bach as a writer of fugues. They resonate well with the Romantic spirit.

What resonated best of all, perhaps, was the combination of factors, mentioned above, which can be heard as teleological, as though driving purposefully toward a goal. The developing variation in section 1 is a preeminently teleological technique. Then new thematic material is introduced step by step—the fluid second subject, the vigorous third, and more. In the great combative stretto and its sequel, the latest comer bids fair to outdo the main subject, seizing the initiative as the race approaches its goal. The *tierce de Picardie* at the end magnificently *is* that goal.

All this—and all subsumed under the ideal aegis of organic form. The Fugue in C-sharp Minor swept Spitta over stormy oceans. It conducted Busoni through a great cathedral:

> In this fugue we seem to be borne upward, out of the crypt of a mighty cathedral, through the broad nave and onward to the extreme height of the vaulted dome. Midway in our flight, the unadorned gloom of the beginning is supplanted by bright ornamentation; mounting to the close, the structure grows in austere sublimity; yet the presence of the unifying idea is felt everywhere—the single fundamental motif leaves its impress on every part.

CHAPTER 5

Contrapunctus 1

The Art of Fugue

Bach prepared *The Art of Fugue* for publication in open score, after having composed it on two staves, in the usual keyboard-music format. The work is a staggering compendium of nearly twenty fugues and canons all based on a single theme, and open-score format—with each voice on its own stave—showed off the contrapuntal devices applied to this ur-theme as clearly as possible. Technical exploits on this scale were unmatched in his own earlier work or that of any other composer then known (then or ever, perhaps). Bach died in 1750, before signing off on *The Art of Fugue,* and for more than two hundred years it was admired and revered, if not always greatly loved, as his last musical testament, undertaken at the end of his life and never completed because of illness and then death.

In the twentieth century, inevitably, his ostensibly abstract score became a very honeypot for performers of every possible sort. It has been recorded by string quartets, orchestras, saxophone quartets, harpsichordists, organists, pianists, and even a consort of seventeenth-century viols. But for this composer learned display was inseparable from practical performance. He wrote the fugues to be played on a harpsichord, and while opinions may differ as to whether that should privilege harpsichord as their ideal performance medium, it should certainly earn them a privileged place on every keyboard player's music stand.

Most of the fugues differ significantly from any Bach had composed earlier. Some are contrapuntally much more complex, loaded with strettos, diminutions, augmentations, and inversions. Some are simpler, for in order to set off the technical virtuosity that was the work's raison d'être, Bach had the extraordinary idea of making its first number a fugue *without* contrapuntal devices. Contrapunctus 1 has neither strettos, diminutions, and so on, nor even countersubjects or recurring episodes. These devices will be introduced only in the succeeding contrapuncti, one by one. In Contrapunctus 1 invertible counterpoint itself is in very short supply. This elemental fugue never modulates beyond the obligatory dominant and subdominant keys.

Of course, as many have pointed out, what Bach accomplished here amounts to a kind of negative virtuosity, for if you set up a fugue subject ahead of time with countersubjects and strettos they will write the fugue for you (some of it, much of it). It is a lot harder to write a convincing fugue without the usual aids. Also extraordinary, and paradoxical, is Bach's decision to open a work like *The Art of Fugue* with a fugue that evokes improvisation. There is actually a written-out cadenza at the end. Paradoxical, because if one improvises a fugue with a simple subject tailor-made for strettos—as this subject is—it is almost perverse to eschew them. Compare the fugal Prelude in E-flat Major from *The Well-Tempered Clavier,* book 1 (pages 71–72).

Example 5

a. Contrapunctus 1

b. Contrapunctus 10

In any case, this most basic of fugues is necessarily also one of Bach's freest and must also be one of his smoothest. This quality is related to an archaic impulse that has often been noted in his later works. Still, the seamless style that he developed for *The Art of Fugue,* starting with its first number, does not sound much like the seamless style of sixteenth-century "Palestrina counterpoint." The contrapuntal lines, consisting mostly of quarter- and eighth-note patterns, move stepwise or by the smallest leaps, and the expectations of eighteenth-century harmony often go unfulfilled. Strong cadences are shunned. While such generalities only begin to explain the almost mesmeric fluency of Bach's late style, they may help sensitize us to contrasts where it is abrogated, such as at those episodes featuring larger leaps *[bars 29–30, 36–40, 49–53],* and at the one really, decisively strong cadence *[bar 74].*

Smoothness is all in this fugue, one feels. It is less articulated or segmented than other fugues—it is hardly segmented at all. The exposition presents the subject and answer uneventfully at regular four-bar intervals (see example 5). No doubt the absence of links or episodes also feels "elemental."

Eventually the surface does begin to ruffle, when in a new exposition the bass steps in on the heels of its predecessor and enters after three bars rather than four *[bar 32]*. This entry—it can be heard as a second stab at stretto, after a previous, premature effort in bars 29–30, what is sometimes called a false stretto—moves rather hastily from the dominant around to the subdominant, twisting and turning the subject oddly. Then the tenor entry, as though checked by the low As in the bass, hesitates, accumulating dissonances—sevenths, ninths, and pungent augmented intervals *[bars 41, 42, 43]*. The soprano in this group of entries emerges as a sort of ethereal climax, led into by another false stretto. The bass drops out, allowing for heightened activity in the remaining voices, like a beating of wings *[bars 48–54]*.

Past the exposition, then, the piece can be seen to grow increasingly complex, though the feeling seems to me not exactly of complexity but of complexities tested out and drifted past, ideas considered and shelved, in a constantly changing improvisational field of a unique kind. Endlessly fertile and quite unstoppable, Bach proceeds spontaneously, almost distractedly, until the piece pulls itself together with one grand gesture, the long dominant pedal in the bass from bar 63 to bar 73.

Literally, of course, the pitch A drops out at bar 66, but in the ear it lasts all the way, so the passage has the effect of a cadenza, an increasingly rhapsodic epilogue during which pitch rises and tension mounts until it is too much to bear—or so we must infer; the buildup is so smooth we had no inkling of impending crisis. This programmatically seamless music literally breaks off, stammers, and finally sinks—truly sinks—to rest. To this aporia some performers add improvised ornaments or flourishes. These cushion the break and seem somehow to humanize the crisis.

• • •

An elemental fugue evoking improvisation, without contrapuntal artifice—this is true, but as one gets to know it better, intriguing details of purposeful counterpoint begin to show up just
below the surface. While Bach may abjure countersubjects,
Benito Rivera has shown in a close analysis how shards of countersubject material, as it were, contribute a pervasive sameness
and tranquility to the free flow (compare, for example, details at
the beginning of bars 7, 11, 15, 42, 51, and 58). There are no
recurring episodes in the ordinary sense, but the two-part canon
in the first episode reappears later under bright new streams of
soprano melody *[bars 17–22, 36–39, 67–70]*. No strettos—but as
we have seen, false stretto used quietly to great effect.

As for Bach's use of the solemn term "contrapunctus," that
accords with his evident intention in *The Art of Fugue* to control
counterpoint as a universal principle, rather than simply the
genre of fugue. Made up of canons and fugues of various kinds
all based on a single theme, the work encompasses more than one
contrapuntal process. (The original title of *Die Kunst der Fuge,*
added to Bach's manuscript in another hand, was *Die Kunst der
Fuga,* "fuga" being the archaic, and by now pedantic Latin term
for imitative counterpoint.) In fact, the project was not the swan
song it was thought to be after its publication in 1751: an early
version exists from as early as 1742–46, and whereas the final
publication remains a torso, the early text looks complete; it is
preserved as an autograph fair copy that could have gone right to
the printer after one or two final touches. This text, though it
received more and more touches over the years and was obviously superseded by the printed version, has its own integrity.
Had Bach died a few years earlier, *The Art of Fugue* would now

Example 6

73

be admired and revered among the great masterworks of Western music in the early version.

For the final version, Bach expanded Contrapunctus 1 beyond its state in the autograph. He also composed two extra fugues for the collection and expanded others, most extensively Contrapunctus 10: see pages 39–49. Originally Contrapunctus 1 closed four bars earlier, prior to the final subject entry that now seals the cadence and bathes it in a wash of fresh color *[bars 74–78]*. The original ending, shown in example 6, is less celebratory, more radical and romantic.

CHAPTER 6

Contrapunctus 10

The Art of Fugue

Contrapunctus 10 from *The Art of Fugue* is a strange composite work of rare beauty, with two subjects.

Section 1: *Bars 1–22*

The singular rhetoric of the first subject—clipped three-note utterances, inverted and contrasted, sinking down/springing up, circuitous/direct, dark/light, with the springing motion retraced, softened, and overshot by a rising scale: this fascinates and mystifies. Also mysterious is the subject's trajectory, beginning on the seventh degree C♯, away from the tonic or dominant notes, the positions taken up by virtually all Bach fugues, and ending—where? Roger Bullivant remarks of this "vague" subject, "left to its own devices the result would hardly be a true fugue." Perhaps, but what matters is not the truth but the multifariousness of fugue. When we need to distinguish between the two subjects of Contrapunctus 10 we can call this one the "enigmatic subject."

Upward scales in eighth notes, spanning the intervals of a seventh and a ninth, echo one another and become an unforgettable feature of Contrapunctus 10. The first of these scales is demarcated by a high C♮ that makes for both climax and also a feeling of constraint, after the scale's initial sense of release (D↗C; bar 3). C♮ also abrogates that initial C♯, so that the music can tilt toward the subdominant—and it is the subdominant, G minor, that accommodates the answer (not the dominant). This casts a sober shadow over what is already a very heterodox fugal exposition.

After the answer the soprano inverts the scale, as though to cradle the two remaining entries of the four-part exposition. These entries confound expectation by arriving in inversion and also in stretto. A link leads to further entries, now in a closer stretto: the recto subject answered by the inversion *[bars 14–17]*. Bach makes it look easy, this utterly improbable contrapuntal feat that throws up new expressive chords on almost every beat. Anyone who doubts the potential for eloquence inherent in the technical devices of fugue, such as inversion and stretto, should be won over by this page. Tovey called it "one of the profoundest and most beautiful Bach ever wrote."

A few bars later there is a tear in the fabric of the composition. The involved history of *The Art of Fugue,* some of which has been sketched on page 37, explains this. Bach's original autograph manuscript transmits Contrapunctus 10 in an early version; both early and final versions became known as soon as the work appeared, since for some reason—perhaps because the versions are so different—both were included in the 1751 publication. While almost all modern editors omit (that is, suppress) the autograph version, it is included in a recent Bärenreiter edition edited by Klaus Hofmann, and also in the venerable Czerny edition of 1838, still in print. It began at bar 23 of the final version. The whole first section, Tovey's profound and beautiful page, was a later addition.

Skip all of bars 1–22 in Contrapunctus 10, omit the bass and alto lines from bars 23–26, make two notational changes, and you have the version of Bach's autograph, except for a few minor variants later.

Section 2: *Bars 23–56*

In the absence of titles for the fugues in Bach's autograph, the early version of Contrapunctus 10 is often designated Fuga 6 (since it occupies the sixth position in that source, not the tenth), and this will be a convenient label for the discussion here.

Fuga 6 began at bar 23 of Contrapunctus 10, so it began with an orthodox exposition, setting forth a subject that inverts the basic theme of *The Art of Fugue* (introduced in Contrapunctus 1; see example 5a, page 35). This neutral-sounding fugue subject could hardly contrast more strongly with the enigmatic subject of Contrapunctus 10.

I have called the exposition of Fuga 6 orthodox, but it is in fact unusually relaxed. The high-flying soprano accompaniment to the answer in the tenor drops out at once, never becoming a regular countersubject. Bach writes free counterpoint for the remaining entries, flowing, seamless, soaring, ever-new. Eventually he settles on a common, even commonplace imitative figure gliding up and down the interval of a fourth in eighth notes, emerging on this occasion from the end of the subject *[bars 33–37]*. The same figure runs over from the fourth entry to the next episode

Example 7

22 26

[38–43]—now ornamented, rather surprisingly, with a trill—
and shapes several others.

How does this sit in Contrapunctus 10, after the extra page has
been added to precede it? Not altogether well. The added voices
in bars 23–26 are crude and unlovely; I cannot believe that Bach
was responsible for this join. (One can play the piece with an eli-
sion, as in example 7.) Also there is something slack about the
succession of ideas. The rich, involuted first section of the work
extends for 22 bars—and 22 bars later the second section has
hardly got past its mild, relaxed exposition; the music is perfect
in itself, but the contrast is unsettling. It is not like Bach to proceed from complex to simple. The relaxed exposition in Fuga 6
feels lax in Contrapunctus 10.

Get over it! as of course we do, when the music picks up
energy with the next entry, in the alto *[bars 44–48]*. In Fuga 6 this
alto entry brought with it low sonorities for the first time, and a
new feeling of gravity, set against the very high, airy beginning.
If we are playing or listening to Contrapunctus 10, we will recognize the counterpoint offered by the tenor at this point. It is the
original enigmatic subject. Or at least, we should recognize it;
with the line hidden away in an inner voice, it could be missed by
listeners and even, possibly, by some players.

And how did this sit in Fuga 6? What in bar 44 of Contrapunctus 10 returns as something old and known, namely the original enigmatic subject, presents itself in bar 22 of Fuga 6 as something new: a new, belated countersubject, a configuration less likely to strike the listener as enigmatic than simply obscure. Absent the first page of Contrapunctus 10, it sounds like another quasi-improvisational addition to the contrapuntal web accruing around the *Art of Fugue* subject. Attention will likely focus at this point on a prominent ascending line in the bass.

Even at the next entry, this obscure countersubject is only beginning to peck its way out of the surrounding counterpoint *[bars 53–56]*.

The difficult birth requires special measures, anticipated by the fast-moving line accompanying the original answer to the *Art of Fugue* subject *[bars 26–30]*. As we have seen, this line did not become a countersubject at that point; it is probably too exuberant to fulfill that function (and the little rhythmic spurt in bar 27 too volatile). It has a special dramatic role to play. In a tentative form, it begins by infiltrating those episodes built on the gliding figure *[bars 43, 49–51]*, hunting for a way back into the fugue after having missed its chance—something it achieves in the next, much more powerful episode.

Bars 56–65

Many so-called episodes in fugues are less than "episodic"; they function not as interludes but as links or transition. Links are often required—from a subject entry to an important cadence, for example. Other episodes are more than episodic; the episode of bars 56–65 drives the fugue. As the voices led by the tenor in bar 56 march around the circle of fifths, the style changes subtly:

the music runs more simply now, in two voices only (some of the time), harmonically repetitious, and more sinewy, with the flowing line itself newly shaped for action.

What the episode is leading to is the emergence of the obscure countersubject (or, the reemergence of the enigmatic subject) into the light of day—its emancipation, in a sense. This happens only when its gnomic opening utterances and then its upward scale, with its always expressive span of a seventh, stand out high in the soprano *[bars 66–70]*. Later it will stand out again in the soprano and also in the bass, that is to say, in both outer voices *[bars 75–79, 85–89, 103–7]*. And emancipation entails a new modality. At bar 63 the high note A in the bass transforms the span of a minor ninth—the heart and soul of the line since its first appearance—into a major ninth (the upward scale G↗A). This is something of a turning point. From here on, remarkably, the piece stays in the major mode for almost the whole of its course; somewhat late, it also turns to new keys, but in a strange way this counts for less than the new modality.

Bars 66–98

We arrive upon the diffused climax of the fugue, a plateau comprising three entries of the combined subjects—the *Art of Fugue* subject and the once-enigmatic, once-obscure, now-emancipated subject—and three episodes. The former subject actually appears each time at the same pitches, in one octave or another (except for one pitch in bar 85), and the episodes bear a strong family resemblance, in that each consists of sequences of two-bar units and each hinges on the same rhythm, an upbeat of three eighth notes. It now becomes clear that Bach fashioned the subjects to combine in invertible counterpoint of many kinds, that is, at many intervals. They go together when one or the other is doubled in thirds or sixths, and even when both are (as nearly happens in bars 102–7). The possibilities are endless. After a slow start, Contrapunctus 10 shows off these contrapuntal devices as clearly and joyfully as any other fugue I can think of (the classic case is the Fugue in G Minor from the *WTC,* book 2).

One cause for the expansive new mood has already been mentioned, the new modality; in later entries the harmony is predominantly major, though the *Art of Fugue* subject itself may maintain its minor-mode form. Another cause is the sensuous, almost buttery quality of the strings of thirds and sixths as they surge together and pull apart, in a sort of mobile double helix. (This texture has been heard before, in bars 16–20. It has reminded one German critic of waltzes by Johann Strauss, Jr.) Once the scale that moves up through a seventh is doubled in thirds, so that it covers a ninth—as in bar 87—it registers expansion rather than constraint, as it did before. The sobriety that marked the first page of Contrapunctus 10 yields to opulence and play.

As to the episodes: though closely related, they grow successively more complex and—Tovey's word—profound.

- *Bars 70–74:* While the first of the three episodes makes use of the gliding scale figure covering a fourth, once again, this always glides up, never down, taking wing up to high C at the very top of Bach's keyboard. Inasmuch as the figure emerges from the conclusion of both the subject and the countersubject *[bar 69],* this episode is heard very directly in reference to the immediately preceding entry, as a celebration of its breakthrough.

- *Bars 79–84:* The second episode blurs its underlying structure by means of a wonderfully skillful lyric gesture in the soprano. It

Example 8

a.

b.

shifts the new three-note upbeat motif—which already feels more purposeful than that of the first episode—to another position in the sequential unit. Example 8a attempts to elucidate this. The actual soprano line from the score has been extracted and printed with stems pointing down, while the strict sequence that was Bach's starting point is shown with dotted stems pointing up.

· *Bars 89–98:* The third episode blurs its sequential nature further. Example 8b, an explanatory score of a different kind, X-rays the full texture to show only notes that I read as functional—the three-note figure of a turn leading to one or more leaps of a fourth—in whatever voices they come. Everything else has been omitted from example 8b . . . except for the murmuring chromatic notes that blur things further yet, and the masterly final transformation of both the turn figure and the leap: these are details I could not leave out. Bach, like his God, is in the details.

What is moving as well as masterly about the third episode is the (retrospective) resonance with the first section of Contrapunctus 10, the added page. In broad terms, the fugue finally regains that page's richness, depth, and intricacy. More specifically, it finally picks up on the resource of inversion explored there, bringing together the opening sinking-down motif and its springing-up inversion—in ornamented versions: perhaps we recognize them as such only when Bach begins to stress the inversion and isolates it by an evocative rest *[bars 94, 96–97]*, as the sequential unit accelerates from two bars to one (indicated in example 8b by extended barlines). The present five-note figure softens and demystifies the original three-note motif.

Bars 98–120

The third episode ends with a sigh. Its material is exhausted or, one would prefer to say, has fully realized its potential and its function by the time of the cadence in bar 98. Though a half cadence, this is perhaps the strongest (least gentle) in the whole piece, echoing similar cadences in bars 22, 56, and 79.

One could hardly conceive of a single episode continuing through the manifest break in bar 98, switching from G minor to B-flat major and from one motif to another. What we have after the cadence is a transition from the cadence to the next entry, a transition that also achieves something like a delicate recapitulation, for bars 98–102 retrace 48–52—down to the tentative intrusion of the flowing figure spanning a ninth that first appeared in 28–31. The flowing figure, which plays so salient a role in the fugue, which reached its apogee in bars 56–66 and has not been heard from since, comes back at full force after the entry *[bars 107–11]*. Then free imitation produces one more beautiful "episode," a new transition to the final entry and the tonic key.

Contrapunctus 10 begins, for me, in mystery and ends with a small mystery of a different sort. The fugue's final entry does return to the "home" key (and mode), D minor, in its first and last bars—with strong F-major and B-flat-major sonorities between, however *[bars 107–14]*. One would have expected some propping-up of the tonic in the closing bars. Yet even as the bass establishes the first strong cadence (A↘D) in the whole fugue, the tenor hesitates to admit finality, and when it does, the piece stops short on the second beat of the final bar.

Even with the fermata that Bach writes on that beat, this makes for the most understated final cadence in *The Art of Fugue*. I struggle to make out what it is saying, or declining to say, about the music it terminates.

Still, more than almost any other Bach fugue, Contrapunctus 10 will reveal new secrets as one plays and studies it again and again. (*The Art of Fugue* "must, indeed, be played many times before its deceptive lucidity can be penetrated," writes Charles Rosen.) The trills at bars 39–41, for example, though they seem surprising at first, can be seen and heard to anticipate another trill at bar 47— a functional trill, in that as written for Fuga 6, it adds definition to the obscure countersubject and confirms a new terminus for it. A similar series of trills also appears at another point in *The Art of Fugue,* in Contrapunctus 3. What is the aesthetic weight, if any, of such interfugue similarities? There are other points in Contrapunctus 10 that seem to reach out beyond the immediate text: at bars 3, 23–28, 31–35 (recalling Contrapunctus 1), and 119–20, to cite a few. To say nothing of the rhythmic identity between those clipped three-note utterances, sinking down/springing up, dark/light, and the hieratic, almost counterintuitive rendition of the *Art of Fugue* subject in Contrapuncti 8 and 11.

To pursue these nuances, one would have to dip into the long-standing debate about "cyclicity" in *The Art of Fugue* as a whole. Is this formidable work to be experienced as a single large cyclic unit, rather than (or in addition to) a series of distinct entities, and if so, just how—what *kind* of cyclicity? One would be drawn to all the other fugues, fugues outside the purview of this short book, and the canons. A prospect to welcome. Do not take Bullivant seriously when he insists that "*The Art of Fugue* is a complete work whose individual numbers make sense only as parts of the whole" and calls the musical evidence for this "overwhelming." There is no such evidence at all for Fuga 6, and only the most tendentious argument can be made for Contrapunctus 10 (or Contrapunctus 1).

CHAPTER 7

Chromatic Fantasy and Fugue, BWV 903

I have taken infinite pains to discover another piece of this
kind by Bach, but in vain. This fantasia is unique, and never
had its like. . . . This work, though of such intricate workmanship, makes an impression on even the most unprac-
ticed hearer if it is but performed at all clearly.

This accolade in 1802 by Bach's first biographer, J. N. Forkel, as
translated into English only six years later, is echoed by George
B. Stauffer, a musicologist who has studied the forty-odd sur-
viving early manuscripts of the Chromatic Fantasy and Fugue to
find out what he can about its chronology—not too much, as is
usually the case with Bach's early music. An early version of the
fantasy dates back to Bach's Weimar years; the fugue may have
been written later.

Stauffer reminds us that this is one Bach composition that
never fell out of sight. Its flamboyance and freedom, pathos and
furor recommended it to the age of *Empfindsamkeit* or sensibility
in the late eighteenth century as well as to several ages of

Romanticism in the nineteenth, resonating in the soundscapes of both the perfected clavichord and the fully developed modern piano. For virtuosi like Liszt and Busoni, this was the only Bach they performed at concerts as originally notated, without being tricked out for the modern instrument. In 1910 Heinrich Schenker put out an edition of the Chromatic Fantasy and Fugue accompanied by a fifty-page monograph, still one of the most comprehensive discussions of any Bach fugue to be found in the musicological literature.

FANTASY

This work owes its fame principally to the fantasy, and of course this is only right. The fantasy is Bach at his most Baroque, Bach at his most extravagant, untrammeled, physical, in your face. The work is a useful corrective for those devotees of the composer drawn especially to the cool technical virtuosity that he liked to display in his later years—in *The Musical Offering, The Art of Fugue,* and works like the Fugue in E Major from *The Well-Tempered Clavier,* book 2. The Bach who daunted traveling virtuosos in contests of improvisation, the seething, fiery, histrionic Bach seldom shows himself so openly as in the Chromatic Fantasy.

The word "untrammeled" may raise eyebrows, since whatever Bach did in the heat of actual improvisation, what he wrote down always has a strong semblance of underlying order and precision. The overall harmonic framework of this particular assault on tonality is simplicity itself. As to rhythm, the ebb and flow of the storm after the opening pair of lightning bolts is controlled by various calculated patterns of three, five, six, and

Example 9

twelve sixteenth notes (not in that order) *[bars 3–20]*, as Schenker showed, and Schenker supplied something similar himself when he composed his own arpeggios for the sequel, in which Bach simply used a shorthand of half-note chords with the instruction *arpeggio [33–48]*. Both Bach and Schenker were using musical notation to induce performances that would sound spontaneously varied.

It is in the arpeggiated passage that Bach begins to bring the most extreme of chromatic chord progressions . . . progressions not to be heard in fugues or Brandenburg Concertos . . . and he continues on the same course in the protracted section, marked "Recitativo," that brings the fantasy to its superb dying close on a long tonic pedal *[49–75, 75–79]*. The music moans and rages with repetitions of short, slow figures, mostly upbeat-downbeat units in which the downbeats are typically the same plain descending step, whereas the upbeats, broken up into patterns of short notes, are wildly and fantastically various (example 9). There are about eleven such figures in the twenty-five bars of the recitative proper, and eight more in the closing passage over the tonic pedal. They would make for rhetorical overkill (even for the Baroque era) if not for Bach's stupefying modulations.

Some commentators find the fugue something of a letdown after the fantasy, but this kind of feeling or judgment relies on false expectations, expectations derived from works like Beethoven's Fifth Symphony where the movements trace a self-consciously teleological course. There is a wide range of relationship between the "movements" that Bach wrote as introductions to fugues—fantasias, preludes—and the fugues themselves. (Sometimes he wrote them at different times and brought them together later; this is apparently the case with the Fantasy and Fugue in A Minor—see page 121—and may be the case here too.) They can be kindred as in the Passacaglia and Fugue in C Minor and the Prelude and Fugue in A Minor from the *Well-Tempered Clavier,* book 2, or mysteriously remote as in E-flat Minor or F-sharp Minor from book 1. E-flat Major in book 1 has been a stumbling block for many. With the Chromatic Fantasy and Fugue, the metronomic motion of the fugue makes a grand overall rhythmic resolution for the fits and starts of the fantasy. As for extravagance and chromaticism, it is as extravagant as a fugue can be and as chromatic as a fast fugue can be.

And whereas some fantasia-fugue pairs stress the contrast between the spontaneous and the composed, in the Chromatic Fantasy and Fugue the sense of improvisation lasts throughout the fugue itself. The radical modulations, the freedom of the figuration, the instability of both the fugue subject and the countersubject, the outbursts of homophony—all of this feels like inspiration found on the spur of the moment. It's hard not to believe that the fugue originated as an improvisation, however much it was tightened up when Bach wrote it down. By writing it down Bach created a text, which players can practice and which critics have been exclaiming over since 1802. Whether he conceived of it as the same *kind* of text as that of a didactic fugue in the *WTC* or *The Art of Fugue*—a text to study and savor at leisure, rather than display as a trophy of improvisation—is another question.

Critics whose method includes "close readings" must always guard against overinterpretation, especially, of course, with texts implicated with performance of one kind or another. Homer and Shakespeare are examples. In music, important examples are jazz and the early keyboard (clavier and organ) works of Bach . . . each presenting different problems: with jazz we have recordings but usually no scores, and with Bach we have scores but can only imagine, never hear the actual improvisation. Such texts are not off-limits to criticism—they just require tact, above all, and a sharp awareness of the limitations of analysis. I do not think my usual critical method would have gotten very far with the Chromatic Fantasy; a little shakily, I come up to speed again with the Chromatic Fugue.

FUGUE

We are of course dealing with a very different genre from *The Well-Tempered Clavier*—music for display rather than study, for spontaneous effect rather than learning or subtlety or refined detail. (Not that this piece lacks its own kind of subtlety.) It seems light-years ahead of other virtuoso fugues for keyboard left by Bach, such as two early works in A minor, BWV 894 and BWV 944, *perpetuum mobile* compositions with subjects in continuous sixteenth-note motion that persists throughout the episodes: see example 2 (page 18). There is also a capacious Fugue in B Minor on a Theme by Albinoni, two versions of which (BWV 951 and 951a) can be found in the back pages of the Bach complete editions, a work with interesting points of contact with the Chromatic Fugue. These early fugues extend themselves by stamina, by means of multiple subject entries and generous (luxuriant, rambling) episodes in various keys. They have no recourse at all to fugal artifice, beyond invertible counterpoint.

The present fugue is a piece of this general type built on a subject with real rhythmic character, to say nothing of involuted melody and harmonic implications far beyond the range of those earlier efforts. On this outing Bach has rejected (or outgrown) the use of sheer whirl for purposes of brilliance and compass. The music achieves what Spitta called its "demoniacal rush" still without recourse to contrapuntal devices such as thematic combinations, stretto, inversion, and the like. Even the countersubject comes and goes casually.

The subject is highlighted at almost all of its appearances by being launched, as it were, by a strong preparatory cadence. Eight bars long, the subject appears eleven times. The piece as a whole runs to 161 bars, nearly five minutes in performance, twelve minutes including the Fantasy.

Subject and Answer: *Bars 1–16*

In a work of this sort, then, the subject counts for all, or nearly all. This subject keeps us on edge throughout, partly because it submits to so much variation, but also because it is so intriguing in itself, even cryptic—as Schenker chose to demonstrate by reducing it to the primal progression A G F E D *[bars 1, 4, 6, 7, 8]*, noting how "the veil is lifted from a wondrous and profound mystery" (example 10a). "What inspired construction!!," he adds.

The mystery lies not in the subject's relatively modest chromaticism but in its ambivalent tonality. If fugue admits any axiom, it is that the subject defines the tonality, but heard in the abstract, this subject veers dangerously toward the dominant;

Example 10

a.

b.

the opening interval A–C *[bars 1–2]* defines not the tonic D
minor but A minor, the dominant key. In this context E–G *[3–4]*
has to suggest the dominant of the dominant, E minor, and E
minor oversteps the range of D minor. (These very harmonies
are spelled out later in transposition *[bars 61–66],* and elsewhere
this first half of the subject is harmonized in many different
ways, seldom in an unambiguous D minor or equivalent key.)
Immediately the B♭ in bar 5 cancels obscurantist E-minor harmony. On B♭ the motif inverts grandly and cascades down to a
very forceful D-minor cadence—compensation (overcompen-
sation, perhaps?) for the mystification before.

We can now see how Schenkerian reduction obscures, sedates,
and indeed betrays the dynamic process central not only to this
fugue's subject, but also to the way it will develop. The B♭
melodic peak will function as a crux globally as well as locally. In
several later subject entries it generates an altogether unusual
canon; in others it precipitates a breakdown of polyphonic texture into thick chords. And a sequence formed from the melodic
peak detonates the biggest explosion in the whole of this highly
combustible composition *[bars 135–40].*

The crux of bar 5 also inflects the fugue's rhythmic structure.

For with the help of an aggressive, dissonant trill in the counter-subject, starting at bar 13, bar 5 earns the force of a downbeat—one that cuts across the normal downbeats, which come on the even bars (starting with bars 2 and 4) and which are strongly affirmed at key points later *[bars 91, 132, 155]*). The rogue accents invigorate the music and contribute to the overall drive.

Every entry of the subject "contains an element of uncertainty," as A. E. F. Dickinson puts it in his book on Bach's fugues. "The fugue is chromatic, then, *per se.*" The answer (a tonal answer) is lucid enough—it traces the intervals D↗G and B♮↗D—but it only comes twice. And the harmonic interval of a seventh between the beginning of the answer and the counter-subject tells us at once that this is a fugue with a pretty short fuse *[bar 9]*. Hans von Bülow in his edition of the Chromatic Fantasy and Fugue changed the answer so as to start on E and cancel the dissonance, understandably infuriating Schenker and fueling one of his many polemics.

Bars 17–97

The long first episode maps out well the scope of the fugue to come *[bars 27–40]*. But after its opening sally of upward fourths in the soprano, it seems to me both weak and peculiar—peculiar in *thematic material:* neither the left-hand thirds nor the motifs in bars 36–40 seem to belong in this fugue—in *harmony:* the over-long circles of fifths—and especially in *form:* the key of F major established with considerable formality, then quitted at once. This looks to me less like a relic of improvisation than scar tissue from early surgery performed on this score, even earlier than the first of the three versions described by Stauffer. Bach may have contemplated an entry in F, though it is hard to see how he could have twisted the subject into the major mode. Another unique and defining feature of the Chromatic Fugue is that it introduces its subject nearly a dozen times with never any mode change.

In entry 4 *[bars 41–49]*, the next after the exposition and the long first episode, what feels like an improvisatory variation of the subject turns out to be the start of a purposeful process, the dismantling of the fugue subject in several stages. Bach varies the subject at the melodic peak, softening it with appoggiatura eighth notes. These expressive diminutions would spell pathos in any other context; here they have a strange grasping effect, and they sound even stranger in entry 5 *[bars 59–66]*—almost uncanny, I feel—when the softened crux is echoed by a canon at the octave between the alto and the soprano (example 10b). Then the rest of the subject simply withers away in both voices. Did Bach consider the cadence of the original subject *too* grand and forceful, too final-sounding for general use? The cadence was already obscured in entry 4, and in all later entries it is virtually smothered with faster matter or omitted altogether.

Entry 5 is contorted further, as to rhythm and harmony alike. A solidly launched bass A in bar 60 shifts accents from the subject's second bar to its first; this regularizes accents on the odd bars—on the melodic peak and the beginning of the canon (the original cadential accent on the even beat has evanesced). The low A also clouds what is actually a tonic entry by means of a strong dominant (reinforced, when the entry returns in this form later, as a pedal *[bar 108]*).

In entry 6 *[bars 76–83]* the subject is undermined some more: for once it is not "launched," the contour of the opening measure is blurred, and the harmony reels dangerously—until the crux,

a turning point once again. The subject cadences in the distant
key of B minor.

And entry 7 marks a further breakdown, yet at the same time
a manifest climax, the Chromatic Fugue's first really extraordinary moment.

The key is E minor (no stranger to this work, as we have seen),
and E-minor harmony is frozen by a dominant pedal B positioned, this time, to stress the subject's second bar *[91]*—an accent
blown out of the water by the accent on bar 94 at the arrival of the
crux, now presented as a cannonade of fat chords of up to eight
notes shattering the three-part contrapuntal texture. Meanwhile
the countersubject, which began decaying in the previous entry,
melts down into continuous sixteenth-note figures—up to the
melodic peak, where its principal idea suddenly reappears, a scale
in marching rhythm (dactyls or anapests). It proceeds down two
octaves in the bass, after ratcheting up the harmony under the
melodic peak into a minor ninth chord. Eventually the marching
bass line will be played by the left hand in octaves, a forecast of
Lisztian bravura that must have fascinated musicians of the nineteenth century *[bars 158–59]*.

For Schenker, the collapse into raw homophony has been
meticulously prepared:

> Bach would not have been the master he was, and indeed
> this profusion of voices would be unconvincing—like a mere
> whim—had he not provided detailed advance preparation of
> the effect he wished to achieve. One should note the uninter-
> rupted, agitated sixteenth notes in bars 87–93 and the threat-
> ening organ point that begins in bar 91! And finally, the most
> inspired stroke: Bach intentionally deletes the last eighth note
> in bar 4 of the subject, as if forcibly stifling the voice-leading's
> drive toward a purely contrapuntal continuation!

Some nineteenth-century editors put the eighth note back, to Schenker's renewed exasperation. Harmony, the subject, the countersubject, and even counterpoint itself break down in the service of climax. Bach's deletion makes for an earthier, stomping quality in the crux, and it is no accident that this is the first time since near the beginning of the fugue, several minutes earlier, that the subject sounds out loud and clear in the soprano.

The episodes, past the first two, have exhibited a flamboyance that rivals that of the subject entries themselves. The episode emerging from entry 4 is a composite of two ideas *[bars 49–58]*, both making a vivid textural contrast with the regular fugal texture (something Bach does not allow in the more compact fugues of the *WTC*). The two ideas—arpeggiated chords on the one hand, and a torrent of continuous sixteenth notes, doubled in thirds or sixths, on the other—also contrast sharply with each other. Then, soon after entry 5, a clear cadence launches a lively episode that is something like a false stretto ahead of entry 6—another flamboyant gesture *[bars 72–75]*. Note the touch of diminution. This tricky preparation helps undermine the entry, along with other factors already mentioned.

Bars 97–161

For all of its arsenal of climax-inducers, entry 7, poised in its distant key, must obviously still be some way from any contemplated final point of rest. What better to defuse the tension at this point—*pour mieux sauter*—than a return of the arpeggios of the texture-inspired episode *[bars 97–106]*. Entry 8 arrives in due course, with fine new elaborations *[107–14]*, and, if the next episode *[115–30]* feels a little generic, what is mainly needed

Example 11

here is a fairly long span of time and general circling of the tonic key. One can feel the fugue approaching its final climax in D minor.

And one has to echo Schenker: what inspired construction! and doubly inspired on account of the music's implication with improvisation. Entry 9, beginning on D and biased toward D by another pedal, turns inevitably toward its proper key, G minor (see example 11). This is the subdominant—definitely *not* where the fugue can end. In an explosive gust of spontaneity, Bach takes the crux and its motif, now loaded up with thick chords and the marching figure, rams it through to the soprano, and sequences the whole complex up from the subdominant past the tonic to the dominant, A. This sequence (E♭ D C B♭ . . . ∫ F E♮ D C♯ . . .) has the effect of trumping the canon that blurred the end of entries 5 and 8. What registers so strongly is the grand, scrunching sound of the two dominant ninth chords, V^9 of iv and V^9 of v *[bars 135, 139]*. While the harmonic progression is not the same as the by now familiar progression leading into the crux, it is not unrelated, and to me it feels like the preordained outcome of that crucial sound, its exultant apotheosis.

If we can imagine Bach improvising the Chromatic Fugue we can also imagine him saving the lowest bass entry for the point directly after this great climax. Very powerful are the successive accents on bars 139 and 140—and while the bass entrance in bar 140 may be premature and impulsive in respect to the sequence of bars 135–38, it is majestically on time in respect to the pedal initiated at bar 132. This *lowest bass* entry, accompanied by a spontaneous new counterpoint of rushing scales, is answered by the *highest soprano* entry, with left-hand octaves below *[bars 154–60]*.

The subject counts for all in this fugue. The superb, impatient flourish at the end stresses the original rhythmic terminus of the subject, as does the afterbeat.

CHAPTER 8

Prelude and Fugue
in E-flat Major

The Well-Tempered Clavier, Book 1

"This Prelude is nothing less than a Toccata and Double Fugue,"
Tovey states at the beginning of his annotation to the Prelude in
E-flat Major from book 1 of *The Well-Tempered Clavier* and later,
on the fugue that occupies bars 25–70 of the Prelude: "The only
theoretical irregularity in this four-part Double Fugue is the
extra semiquaver figure in the soprano of bar 26 which antici-
pates the genuine answer in bar 27." Tovey's instinct was to
defend this fugue from unspecified charges or suspicions that it
lacked theoretical "regularity"—this from a writer who cam-
paigned tirelessly against false premises in the music theory of his
day. But he was off the mark in this case. Also troublesome is
David Schulenberg's hearty reference to "full-fledged fugue subjects" in this work (though he should be taken seriously, I think,
when he says it may be the greatest prelude in book 1 of the *WTC*).

A terminological point: a toccata, for the seventeenth century,
was a segmented composition consisting of a number of free
improvisatory sections and contrapuntal ones that may or may

not count, from our standpoint, as actual "fugues." Bach in his early years wrote eight or nine such toccatas, large-scale pieces for clavier and organ, which generally include two free sections and two fugues. By the eighteenth century the genre had coalesced into the toccata and fugue: a single introductory movement, often free-standing, and a single fugue. In Bach's "Dorian" Toccata and Fugue in D minor for organ, there is little that is improvisatory in the concerto-form first movement or in the exceptionally rigorous fugue.

The other so-called Toccata and Fugue in D minor, a stormy piece once well known in Stokowski's orchestral transcription (but quietly dropped out of the 2000 remake of *Fantasia),* is a toccata—its actual title—in the seventeenth-century tradition, consisting of three big sections, all of them improvisatory and flamboyant: introduction, fugue, and conclusion. The Prelude in E-flat Major also belongs in this genre. It has one improvisatory section with two short subsections—I shall call them toccata fragments—and a large double fugue exhibiting so many free, improvisatory, "irregular" features that it could never have found its way into the *WTC* as a "fugue," only as part of a special prelude. (David Ledbetter, in his recent book *Bach's Well-tempered Clavier,* reminds us that toccata was an alternative name in the seventeenth century for one kind of prelude. The "Dorian" Toccata and Fugue is called Prelude and Fugue in some early sources.)

If we are ever to imagine what actually happened when Bach improvised a fugue, it will be with the help of the Prelude in E-flat Major, which I take to be a (brilliantly) enhanced record of keyboard improvisation. Whereas the subject of another improvisatory fugue, the Chromatic Fugue in D Minor, responds uniquely to a unique fantasia, the main subject of this one partakes of the commonest of clay, endlessly remolded. Bach generated fugues with this material at the keyboard over and over again, I would assume, and when he came to put together *The Well-Tempered Clavier* decided it was time to write down his latest version. Even after segregating it from the twenty-four official fugues, he must also have disciplined it carefully to accord with its new canonic status.

PRELUDE

Toccata Fragments: *Bars 1–25*

Bach is tracing a myth of genesis, the emergence of order from inchoate, improvisatory stirrings. A highly developed double fugue will be brought into being by two distinct toccata fragments, remnants or evocations of keyboard improvisations in which the fugue's two subjects are adumbrated, one by one. Thematic relations between segments of a toccata are a typical feature of the genre, not a special innovation or refinement by Bach.

Yet as written down in the first toccata fragment, the improvisatory gestures freeze *[bars 1–10]*. The counterpoint is of the sort that lies under the keyboard player's hand—a flowing figure in sixteenth notes repeating itself insistently—until the figure suddenly accelerates strictly, without any change in its shape. It is on the point of becoming dangerously rigid when a flourish leads to an abrupt cadence; the whole thing lasts only ten bars. (The passage was less rigid, incidentally, in an earlier version of the prelude.)

The second toccata fragment brings to mind Bach's fame as an organist and the many calls he received to test out and vet new instruments. The first thing he did on these occasions, according to his early biographer, Forkel, was to draw out all the stops and play with the full organ. "He used to say in jest that he must first of all know whether the instrument had good lungs." One can associate this routine with the slow-moving, dense, pensive style of this music, which indeed sounds a lot better on the organ than on harpsichord or clavichord.

However, all of the organ stops are surely not pulled out. And this meandering search for rich sonorities conceals (or embraces) a purposeful motivic process. The counterpoint at the start formulates the main stretto that will be used in the double fugue—a primitive motif involving an upward leap of a fourth in close stretto at the lower fourth or upper fifth *[bars 10, 11–12, 16–17]*. The bass expands this motif into foreshadowings of the main fugue subject *[bars 12–13, 16–17, 18–20]*.

Both toccata fragments come to the same formal half cadence on the dominant, B♭. The fugue's opening subject entry is in the dominant. From the second fragment Bach derives the main, slow subject of the upcoming double fugue, and from the first—from its insistent motif—he spins the other, faster subject, stiffening the end of it to provide more distinct rhythmic definition. Even the one minor-mode tonality hinted at in the toccata *[bar 16]* proves to be prophetic, when C minor emerges as the most prominent secondary area in the double fugue.

Double Fugue: *Bars 25–70*

This fugue should not really be construed structurally apart from its improvisatory attendants. Almost the whole composition seems driven by much the same melodic idea, presented again and again starting from the same pitch, B♭: the primitive motif B♭↗E♭ D | C (B♭) of the second toccata fragment, or its expansion as the main fugue subject B♭↗E♭ D ↗| G (F).

Both melodic configurations also appear starting from other pitches, of course. But most of the entries starting from B♭—ten of them in all—stand out for one reason or another and so can be experienced as structural:

- *Bars 10, 25, and 49:* Entries start up again after parallel half cadences that settle heavily—and, at bar 49, somberly—on B♭, the dominant of E-flat major.
- *Bar 42:* The entry stands out because the countersubject returns after a fairly long absence.
- *Bar 61:* Organ music is evoked, once again, in particular a climactic device well known from the "St. Anne" Fugue—a thinning of texture toward the end of an organ fugue, with slowly descending high voices that set off a grand subject entry low in the pedals, an entry that reintroduces and supports the full texture.
- *Bar 64:* Here the subject stands out because it is in the soprano, expands further to become G↗| C B♭↗E♭ D↗G♭ | F E♭D | E♭, and is at the same time normalized, in that it finally comes to rest on the tonic note, E♭.

There is special point to the word "finally" in this situation. Both subjects of this fugue are treated very freely. Both (to put it another way) are very unstable. The main subject as it appears in the tonic, in the form E♭↗A♭ G ↗| C B♭, asserts the tonality weakly because it ends on the dominant and on a weak beat—and even this much definition is denied to it much of the time, for although the beginning entry (B♭↗E♭ D↗| G F) promises that F is destined to sink to E♭ *[bar 27]*, this closure is usually evaded.

The tonality vacillates; the big bass entry near the end simply hangs on to its penultimate note, G, skipping (or skidding past) F altogether *[bars 62–63]*. Only after this does an extended soprano entry guide the subject down from G♭ and F to E♭—a clear tonic at long last.

The tonal equivocation in this work becomes a nice problem for the music theorist who might wish to engage with its network of nuances. In broader terms it matters to any player or listener, for it is probably the equivocal, open-ended subject that contributes more strongly than anything else to a sense that the rambling, improvisatory quality of the second toccata fragment lasts throughout the rest of the composition. In this "free" quality the E-flat Prelude fugue is quite unlike the *WTC*'s labeled fugues, as has already been noted.

Equally unstable, the second, faster subject of this fugue appears as many times freely as strictly (five) and drops out of the composition well before the end. Yet the fugue is permeated by the toccata's short flowing figure in its original, undeveloped form. This appears in nearly every bar, often more than once. (The figure even elbows its way an extra time into the initial fugal exposition—this was Tovey's "theoretical irregularity.") Rigor that bordered on the obsessive in the 10-bar first toccata fragment makes good sense in the 45-bar fugue, or so it seems to me—a compositional feat to reckon with.

Strict and free. The fugue's opening exposition is another free feature, in the deepest sense: the main subject appears in only three of the four voices, the second subject in only two *[bars 25–34]*. And immediately after this the fugue plunges unexpectedly toward the mediant, G minor *[bar 35]*. From here on ruminative strettos in minor keys stamp this music with unusual gravity.

Example 12

Almost every entry of the main subject appears as part of a stretto—typically in the form first heard in the second toccata fragment—and the more intense junctures also involve false strettos. Thus the concatenation of upward fourths in bars 41–44 builds up such pressure that counterpoint loses hold and the voices coalesce into a singular outburst of regal passion. This is an amazing moment, more like the opening chorus of a cantata of penitence or supplication than a keyboard fugue. Doesn't this count as an "irregularity"? One feels an aftershock in bar 52.

The free flow of this fugue allows for scarcely any strong cadences; the half cadence in bar 49 marks the point where Bach sights the tonic and begins a long buildup to a sustained climax. Characteristically, the tonality is deflected, and the strettos proceed in a discursive, rolling motion, almost somnolent, like a blind giant (though the four entries in bars 53–59 march in strict order, at successive intervals of a bar and a half). The most intense stretto of all comes in the highest register, a de facto one-bar stretto at the unison: see example 12.

Another pileup of strettos achieves resolution, this time by gestures not of passion but pain *[bars 64–70]*. The climactic soprano entry clutches up and up but cannot reach G, only Gb. Supported by Cb a moment later, this echoes that somber Gb lodged in our memory from the half cadence at bar 49, the fugue's central cadence.

FUGUE

At one time many musicians were disturbed by the mood sequence from the Prelude in E-flat with its four-part double fugue to the much lighter, three-voiced Fugue in E-flat that comes next. Riemann in his book on the *WTC* dismissed the latter as superfluous, a "harmless merry postlude," and Keller practically begged readers of *his* book to approach the two pieces individually, not as a pair. Busoni heartlessly replaced this book 1 fugue with the weightier Fugue in E-flat Major from book 2— thus joining one fugue to another fugue "vaguely but distressingly similar in theme," as Tovey noted sourly. For Tovey it was axiomatic that Bach valued clear contrasts between preludes and fugues more than "casual resemblances" of thematic content.

Certainly the contrast between the fugue and the prelude is more than a matter of mood or tone. Whereas the prelude is exceptional in never modulating to the dominant, the fugue hits the dominant hard as early as bar 2. (This is one of the few fugues in the *WTC* with a modulating subject.) Likewise, the tidy A B A structure of the fugue contrasts with the at first discursive, then heavily climax-oriented trajectory of the prelude.

Yet there is a good deal more than "casual resemblance" between the main subject of the double fugue of the prelude and the subject of the "official" fugue; the first half of the latter subject, which is so clearly (pointedly?) demarcated from the second half, is little more than an ornamentation of the former. There is also an obvious echo of the end of the prelude in the fugue's last subject entry, in the alteration of G to G♭ *[bar 34]*. C♭ comes not long after. I also experience clearly the parallelism between strong submediant (C-minor) areas in both works.

Ledbetter points to the subtle role of chromaticism in this work, starting with the (piquant, if not adjacent) clash between A♭ and A♮ at the very beginning and culminating in the alteration of G to G♭ near the end, as just mentioned. This culmination is also a witticism, I think, hinting at a rhetorical or improvisatory flourish muffled before its time. "Fugue in the seventeenth century was regarded as a play of wit, not pedantry, and as with Haydn, so with Bach, the tradition continued." For a witty place in the otherwise sober prelude, see bar 67, where Bach brings the ever-present flowing figure from the toccata once—just once— in inversion.

CHAPTER 9

Fugue in E Major

The Well-Tempered Clavier, Book 2

The conventional form diagrams and tables of music pedagogy give or can give the wrong impression of an art we experience as a process (or stasis) in time. Diagrams intrude on listening by asserting their own kind of direct linearity. They announce major articulations and endings ahead of time, before they have been suggested in sound, and offer unambiguous ground plans for patterns in time that are existential and often tenuous. But with some misgivings I do offer a tabular analysis in this case, to make what seems to me a capital point about this famous and famously beautiful fugue, "one of the clearest in intention ever written," according to A. E. F. Dickinson in his book *Bach's Fugal Works.*

What Dickinson seems to have been alluding to in his gnomic way (but nobody else talks about it at all) was the unusually strong segmentation of this music into long parallel phrases. Phrases of virtually the same length, demarcated by very sonorous cadences, all start in the same way, with closely knit four-part expositions of the subject. Past the opening, these expositions

Phrase number	*Number of bars*				
1	9	Exposition	→	half cadence	(dominant of E: I)
2	8	Stretto 1	→	cadence in C-sharp minor	(vi)
3	8	Stretto 2	→	cadence in F-sharp minor	(ii)
4	13	Stretto 3 (varied subject) *leading without a strong cadence to*			
		Stretto 4 (diminished subject) + more entries			
			→	cadence in G-sharp minor	(iii)
5	9	Stretto 5: return of stretto 1 + extra bass entry			
			→	final cadence in E	(I)

are pressed into various strettos; after a time the rich cadences begin to echo one another, like the slow chime of the big gong in a gamelan. A very large hypermeter makes itself felt, at least vaguely comparable to that of a composition in theme-and-variation form—a theme followed by several variations. Segmentation of this kind is particularly impressive in so compact a composition.

Parallelism breaks down in phrase 4, of course, under the pressure of events, when an extra stretto (stretto 4) stirs up the fugue's climax of involution. Yet this single extended phrase also begins with a stretto in all four voices, stretto 3 *[bars 23–26]*—and for a while, if you are not looking at a diagram, you could take it for another "variation."

Phrase 1: *Bars 1–9*

Starting in the bass, the exposition proceeds through successively higher and higher voices, in a hypermeter of three whole notes: see example 13a. Both features make for a feeling of quiet

Example 13

a.

countersubject

b.

grandeur, offset by the more active countersubject. The rising scale in quarter notes in this countersubject, the eighth-note snap B↘F♯↗B, and the syncopated half notes—these will all work magic over the course of the Fugue in E Major. What is left of the phrase consists of a spacious cadence on the dominant, a peaceful gesture, coming as it does so close to the beginning of the composition.

Phrase 2 (stretto 1): *Bars 9–16*

The next phrase brings the first of the strettos. Stretto 1, like the others, is laid out symmetrically in voice pairs: two voices are introduced as a pair at a close stretto interval—a very close one in this case, a single whole note—followed after a time by the other two, in the same disposition. The music does not depart from the tonic key.

The rest of phrase 2 is saturated by the countersubject, generally with the characteristic eighth-note snap smoothed out and made lyrical—a free augmentation. This burgeons into an ample canon or stretto of its own, in all four voices; Bach's strategy is to stress the countersubject at the beginning of the fugue, drop it out of the middle, and restore it in its integral form at the end.

Two strettos this soon in the piece would seem to presage some complexity, but both the augmentation and the way the soprano is laid out tend to minimize any potential developmental energy. So at the second cadence there is again an unusually peaceful feeling at an early point in the proceedings, in spite of the modulation to C-sharp minor. (This feeling may owe something to the long, almost dreamlike line in ascending quarter notes that can be traced in bars 12–15 by shunting back and forth among the octaves: sixteen steps from E♯ up to G♯.)

Phrase 3 (stretto 2): *Bars 16–23*

In stretto 2 the voices in the pairs are less closely bound, at a stretto interval of two whole notes.

It is time for intensity to mount, thanks first of all to tonal ambiguity—the stretto comes *on* E major but *in* the key of C-sharp minor—and then to harmonic and rhythmic tensions inherent in two new countersubjects. (Neither will be heard after this phrase.) One of them features a chromatic progression, the other syncopations and a series of repeated eighth-note turns *[bars 16–17, 17–19, 19–20]*. Partly because the syncopations continue into the cadence, the fugue's second cadence in a minor key, F-sharp minor, sounds more profound than the first, in C-sharp minor, not only lower.

Phrase 4 (strettos 3 and 4): *Bars 23–35*

The voices engage at the shortest stretto interval yet, a half note, and the subject appears in variation.

The fugue is growing more intricate and intense, and to bring matters to a head, Bach throws the whole book at us (gently). The mode switches: the stretto brings the subject four times in the minor mode. The stretto interval tightens. The variation itself is so subtle that Roger Bullivant in his book on fugue admits that he caught on to it only after reading the commentary by Tovey! Tovey haughtily treated such variation procedure as a commonplace in Bach's work, but in fact the thematic manipulation on this occasion stands out for its originality and suavity.

A little figure consisting of two upward steps in quarter notes, emerging from the varied subject itself (see example 13b), mutters away in various voices throughout the stretto, even before the second voice materializes. As to rhythmic intricacy, not only has the music slipped into continuous quarter-note motion, with the help of the figure just mentioned, but the surfaces are ruffled by a hint of triple meter in the varied subject (example 13b). Each of the previous strettos has led fairly quickly to a strong cadence, and this one seems headed for another, in bar 27.

But this is the point where parallelism among the phrases breaks down. The cadence is interrupted (made "deceptive"), and what interrupts is a new stretto, of the subject in diminution.

Bullivant writes as follows about diminution in fugal writing: "It is not a very common device; while intensifying the movement, it has also the tendency to make the subject disappear into the flow of the counterpoint." Just the reverse happens here. The counterpoint has already begun to flow more smoothly from the beginning of phrase 4, and this quarter-note flow is now articulated and, as it were, rationalized by the diminution of the subject into quarter notes. The rhythm clears up, and so does the harmony; perhaps the most beautiful moment in this beautiful fugue comes as the diminished stretto in the alto—and stretto

Example 14

a.

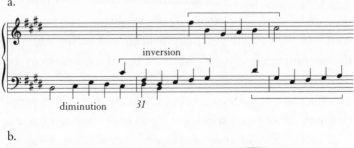

inversion

diminution   *31*

b.

36

c.

38

has never sounded more natural—pulls away from the minor mode toward B major *[bar 27].*

We seem to be hearing a new voice, a more intimate speaking voice, volatile and emotional. The eventual response in bars 34–35 is the most profound cadence yet, in the mediant, G-sharp minor. The intermediate cadence in 27–28, the fugue's first in the dominant key, long awaited, is much slighter—radiant, all the same.

In bar 29, the also radiant ascent to E in the soprano can be heard as an outcome of the upward-step figure—and if it also recalls the original countersubject, that is no accident, as will become clear in a moment. A fifth subject entry in diminution, in the bass, after four in the stretto, is answered in the tenor with another unique thematic manipulation *[bars 30–31].* This answer, at the same time interval as before, brings the subject much changed: inverted, with the opening note abbreviated (from a half note to a quarter) and the opening interval expanded, from the putative step G♯–F♯ to the leap C♯↘F♯.

Described in words or referred to a score (example 14a), this analysis may appear forced: inversion, diminution, abbreviation, expansion . . . To the ear, however—to my ear—the transformation is not only convincing but also climactic in a quite wonderful way; it is exactly because of the hyperbolic expansion of the launch that we recognize the figure as an inversion—as an answer—at all. Against the whirl of this subject/answer pair in diminution, and the rich, almost passionate sequence that emerges from it, the subject in its normal time values can slip by almost unnoticed *[bars 30–32]*.

Phrase 5 (stretto 5): *Bars 35–43*

Bach moves directly from the G-sharp-minor cadence to the tonic key E. Stretto 5 recapitulates stretto 2, with the alto, tenor, and bass entering on the identical pitches at the same time interval, and the soprano at the correct pitch also. With this difference: the soprano waits before sweeping in at a higher octave, like a diva with a catch in her voice; the abbreviation of the subject's opening note in bar 39 makes a comparable effect to that of bars 30, 31, and 32. With this superb entry the highest voice at last reaches its highest register, which it has not even come close to since the start of the fugue.

Two bars later an extra entry, in the bass again—extra, after the four entries of the stretto—leads to the final cadence *[bars 40–43]*. Of all the bass entries, this one reaches lowest down and in doing so gives us something we have been wanting badly for a long time without knowing it: as amends for the subject's boring ending on its opening note, the line continues to sink down through an entire octave, coming to rest on the low tonic. The soprano entry beforehand has done something complementary.

These two final entries, high and low, cap and close a phrase that recapitulates matter more closely than usual even in those Bach fugues that can be said to have recapitulations, or something like them. Back in the tonic key, elements are retrieved and brought together from both phrases 1 and 2—both of which, of course, asserted the tonic. From phrase 2, the first of the strettos returns (up to a point) exactly, and from phrase 1, the original countersubject.

The latter returns right away with new vibrancy in the soprano, at a higher register than ever before, ushered in by the diminished inverted subject: see example 14b. (This combination of subject and countersubject could be the most brilliant of all the fugue's thematic manipulations; one can also hear it incorporating the upward-step figure as expanded to the rising scale from G♯ to E, in bar 29.) The eighth-note snap E↘B↗E, a vivid yet serene reminder of the now distant past, proliferates in the graceful tumble of bars 38–39 and its sequel. Bach reaffirms the thematic combination in the alto and then in the tenor with the opening notes E and D♯—the "correct" inversion notes, at last—transposed down an octave (see example 14c).

They have to be transposed down because otherwise the left hand cannot reach them, but if the fugue were sung rather than played they would certainly be moved back up—and this fugue has been found to be eminently singable. More than one musician had tried it out on an a capella choir before the Swingle Singers dressed it up with scat syllables and a drum track on a hit record of forty years ago, still in the catalog.

One more unique thing about the Fugue in E Major is worth noting: the vacuity of its subject. Does any other Bach fugue make use of anything so primitive? David Ledbetter in his book on the *WTC* traces the long history of this stretto-happy six-note configuration in early fugal writing. It is stock matter in the classic ricercars and fantasias of Johann Jakob Froberger, in the *Ariadne Musica* of J. C. F. Fischer—Bach's model for a series of fugues in all the keys, though Fischer can only coax his club-footed Theseus through twenty turns of the harmonic labyrinth, not twenty-four—and in the principal music textbook of the time, the *Gradus ad Parnassum* of Johann Joseph Fux. Even the striking sectionalization of the Fugue in E Major can be seen as Bach's response, supremely artistic and perhaps slightly ironic, to Fux's elementary rules for fugal structuring.

He would never have chosen such a subject for the *WTC* without meaning to show how common clay could be not so much molded, drawn out, and worked up as humanized, inspirited. For it is not so much the technical virtuosity of this work that impresses—the systematic strettos, diminutions, augmentations, inversions, and other thematic manipulations—as its extraordinary grace and serenity. The Prelude in E Major being marvelous in its own way, this prelude and fugue has levitated out of the *Well-Tempered Clavier* onto Dickinson's and many other people's manifest of music to be taken along to the once-proverbial desert island, to the soon-to-be-discovered habitable, and therefore musicable planet in outer space.

Dickinson played it on camp pianos in World Wars I and II

and called it "the best safeguard, in abstract sound, of the belief that whatever may happen to the contrary there will always be a sane world to make and keep, and incidentally—observe the cadence—a free England." Anglophobes can play a different ornament in place of the four-eighth-note Rule Britannia figure in bar 42, or just quarter notes G♯ A (in which case dot the B).

CHAPTER 10

Fugue on "Jesus Christus unser Heiland"

Clavierübung, Book 3

The Fugue on the chorale "Jesus Christus unser Heiland" counts as the rogue fugue in the present selection, perhaps, though one likes to think of every Bach fugue as rogue or phoenix or *unicum* in its own special way. It comes from the organ volume of the *Clavierübung,* Bach's comprehensive publication of his keyboard works, which he issued serially and at leisure over the years 1726 to 1742. Volumes 1, 2, and 4 transmit well-known works like the Partitas, the Italian Concerto, and the "Goldberg" Variations.

In volume 3, less well known, a massive organ prelude and the grand "St. Anne" Fugue serve as bookends for a shelf of chorale preludes of many different kinds, based on chorales associated with the Lutheran catechism. Eight hymn melodies are each set twice, first as a large-scale piece for full organ with pedals, and then as a smaller setting for the manuals alone. Included in the collection is a little set of two-part inventions—Bach's somewhat odd name for them is "Duetto"—which are often played on the harpsichord. The series of *manualier* chorales also can be played on any keyboard instrument (harpsichord, clavichord, or piano), not only organ.

The heading "Fuga super 'Jesus Christus unser Heiland'" would have categorized the piece for musicians of the time. The chorale fugue or fughetta is a special keyboard genre going back to the seventeenth century. A motif taken from the first line of a chorale, usually with some ornamentation, becomes the subject of a fugue, a fugue that ends with the entire first line presented in its simplest form in augmentation, as though rising above (or sinking below) the fray. Improvising fugues was part of the organist's stock in trade, and in a chorale prelude we can picture him ruminating fugally on the main music of the hymn he is about to accompany, arriving at a weighty statement of it as a prompt to the congregation to start singing.

The present fugue is an almost unimaginably transfigured version of this genre, which Bach also resuscitated and handled less radically elsewhere in the *Clavierübung*. It must also be one of the most dramatic, in the sense of eventful, fugues Bach ever wrote. The drama begins in a mood of sobriety and pain and ends in transcendence. The "events" of this chorale fugue can serve as a focus for my discussion.

The subject comes from line 1 of a short catechism hymn sung for the Eucharist. Bach altered the fourth note of the melody from B♭ to B♮ (see example 15), though he set the same chorale in several other works (including the other chorale prelude on the same tune in the *Clavierübung*) without making this alteration; he had to make it here because he wanted to write a stretto fugue, and certain of the strettos require the alteration. The alteration itself required or rather allowed Bach to write interesting, often wrenching dissonances (see bars 7, 9, 11, 16, 25, 38, 44, 57,

Example 15. Chorale "Jesus Christus unser Heiland"

and 58). The organist and organ historian Norbert Dufourcq, one of the few commentators who seem to have been struck by this work, speaks of its *chromaticisme tourmenté*.

Section 1: *Bars 1–19*

At the beginning of this stretto fugue, two four-part expositions of the subject in stretto actually overlap *[bars 1–11, 10–19]*—a sober, oppressed, dense inception. Originally the stretto answer follows the subject after six beats, and indeed the whole of the exposition falls into a regular $\frac{3}{2}$ meter, the episode between the tenor/alto and soprano/bass pairs of entries lasting for six beats also.

The next exposition is rhythmically much less regular, indeed convoluted, willfully so, since in the first entry pair the answer follows after only one beat, and in the second pair after two beats. Since these extremely tight strettos do not "work" very naturally, we get a lot of tormented chromaticism.

A countersubject, in its original form or in exact inversion, continues through each of the brief episodes in this section of the

Example 16

fugue, overlapping the entries *[bars 5–7, 13–16]*—a bit of unobtrusive virtuoso workmanship typical enough of this composer. But here, I believe, the music itself is intended to be as unobtrusive as the technique. The listener or even the player cannot be particularly conscious of this countersubject as such, with motion as characterless as this. All one really hears is a rhythmic layer—eighth notes against the heavy quarters of the subject (example 16a). This material has yet to reveal its true function, as a matrix for the evolution of something new and more important.

Section 2: *Bars 19–30, 30–36*

Typically in fugues—though not always, of course—a strong structural cadence, such as the cadence in the dominant C minor at bar 19, prepares a subject entry. This does not happen here. A new section, devoted primarily to the countersubject, begins with intimations of new energy conveyed by a short eighth-note upbeat figure, an upward leap of a fourth taken from the subject (G↗C, C↗F, F↗B♭). The section continues for sixteen bars—almost as long as the fugue's first section.

The "event" here is the transformation of that innocuous countersubject into something newly distinctive and expressive. In effect, we get a new countersubject, and for congregations that had known their hymns since childhood it immediately recalled the last line of "Jesus Christus unser Heiland" (see examples 15 and 16b); the last line of this hymn is doubly memorable as by far the highest and freest of the four. The ordinary chorale fugue treats line 1 of its chorale; Bach's Fugue on "Jesus Christus unser Heiland" treats line 1, then line 4, then brings lines 1 and 4 together in its unique conclusion. Once again Bach presents the material in both recto and inverted forms, in the high voices *[bars 23–27],* while the low voices issue a knot of subject entries in close stretto. To hear these as the primary element rather than as a backdrop would hardly be possible, however; the low entries are obscured, as none others are in this fugue. (The bass entry starts not at its ordinary pace but with a momentary diminution—the new eighth-note upbeat C↗F—and the tenor entry blurs as a result of a false stretto in the alto, G↗C *[bars 23–24].*)

As for the transformation process, example 16b does not attempt to trace but can perhaps suggest the subtlety involved.

The first element of change is rhythmic: the abbreviation of the original four-note pattern, as in bars 3 and 5, to a more shapely and distinctive pattern of three, as in bars 21 and 23. The second element is melodic: the repeated emphasis on the affective semitone Db C in the three-note figure C Db C, which then shrinks into just the two notes Db C: a truly Bachian stroke of high pathos.

The fugue almost grinds to a halt, as though overcome, on a low pedal C lasting for two and a half bars *[bars 27–29]*. A pedal on C in the key of F minor ought to presage the end of the piece, or at least the end of a major passage, but the music surges up, agitated by sixteenth notes, till it reaches an extraordinary moment of collapse and release as the pedal evaporates and the countersubject attains its highest point yet, F Gb F in the soprano. The place is both a climax of pathos—the highest Gb in the composition so far—and a consolation, because of a new stage of melodic transformation that leads to a placid new cadence. A beautiful long, relaxed episode, at first in only three parts, mulls over the major-mode sonorities that have been denied to this fugue until now. The countersubject remains in the spotlight. Contrasting episodes are routine in Bach's fugues; what makes this one such an event is its dramatic, even melodramatic highlighting.

The countersubject has been transformed—has come into its own, rather—and now it disappears, or rather, it makes a strategic exit. At the cadence, listen to the soaring upward-fourth leaps in the tenor and the bass *[bar 34]*, the bass Gb also echoing the earlier climax on the high Gb *[34, 30]*.

Section 3: *Bars 36–56*

By the time of its second large structural cadence, the fugue has ranged far from its sober, depressed, dense inception. The subject has been lost. Even the tormented minor mode and its chromaticism have been forgotten, until the cadence twists us back to B♭ minor, the subdominant. Now the piece shakes itself and returns to its origins, in a new intense round of entries in stretto, entries of a very different character.

Having already challenged the subject, as it were, with two (related) countersubjects, Bach now does something different. He unleashes a whole arsenal of technical devices to destabilize the subject—and disorient the listener. The soprano hiccups and leaps up to an entry placed at the very top of the keyboard, leaving a gap in the middle of the texture *[bar 37]*. Following the previous alto entry after five beats (an odd, not the usual even number), this raises a specter of false accentuation to taunt the listener who remembers her catechism: *Je-SUS Chri-STUS un-SER Hei-EI-LAND.* The alto and tenor engage in frantic chromatic gesturing. Sixteenth-note figures enter and the bass begins to dance in a de facto $\frac{3}{4}$ meter, for six bars (equivalent to four and a half bars in $\frac{4}{4}$: see example 16c). A clear motif emerges, F E♭ D | E♭↗A♭↘D, joined in canon by the soprano: E♭ D C | D↗G↘C. (This motif, the most important new thematic element in the fugue, had already been teased out of the end of the subject in bars 39–41, by the alto. There is a beautiful forecast of it in bars 25–26.) Although Bach will now sometimes fit this motif loosely in with the subject *[bars 39–40, 43–44, 51]*, he will conspicuously *not* develop it into a new consistent countersubject.

For a considerable time the counterpoint remains loose and fantastic. Two rather isolated subject entries in the bass *[bars 44–46, 50–53]* are spaced out by episodes *[41–43, 46–50, 53–56]*, and a larger rhythmic module begins to assert itself, for the entries and episodes all occupy about the same time span. In the first two of the episodes just mentioned the new motif proliferates, and in the third it generates a swift new figure, C↗E♮ F↘ | B♭↗E♭. This forms a canonic sequence driving toward a cadence.

Bars 57–67

Again the subject is losing ground; its stretto energy seems all played out. But there is still one exceptional contrapuntal tour de force to come. The next, next-to-final event in this fugue answers to the generic dictate of the chorale fugue: the return of the tonic key and the apparition of the fugue subject augmented to half notes.

As if augmentation were not an event momentous enough to terminate so intense a composition—or as if in the history of the genre chorale fugue the very device had worn thin—when Bach brings the subject in augmentation in the soprano he brings it simultaneously in the tenor in its normal note values. By this time he has contrived strettos at nearly every possible time interval—after one, two, four, five, and six beats. Think of this combination of subject and augmentation as yet another stretto of a sort, a stretto at time-interval zero, after no beats at all.

Not only this: the subject-augmentation combination is further overlaid by the countersubject, returning after an absence of twenty bars, reminding us at the end of the fugue of the end of the chorale, and creating a sublime clockwork of continuous eighth notes geared to the characteristic quarter-note motion, geared in turn to the half-note master meter of the new augmentation. Instead of increasing the density of the original rhythmic layering of quarter notes and eighths, the terminal extra layer seems to clear it up and makes it lucid. The countersubject reasserts itself in one form or another (sometimes, of course, in inversion) in almost every bar of the augmented entry. Bar by bar—this is the same frequency as in the beautiful central episode.

The whole is whitened. Sixteenth notes are leached out of the texture. The music repeats itself like a mantra. And the evaporation process at the very end—the cadence glimmering away as in a dust cloud—has to count as the last striking event in this strikingly eventful fugue. We are not usually asked to track so many changes of mood in a fugue; the process here is fascinating, dizzying. After all of the changing the music ends with transcendence. I glimpse in our fugue a not-arbitrary series of what Robert Schumann called *Seelenzuständen*—"soul conditions":

The soul in torment . . . *andante e mesto*
Anguished transformations . . . *sempre più mesto*
A vision of grace . . . *tranquillo subito*
Rejection: fantasies, frenzies . . . *un poco agitato, quasi scherzando (ma in tempo)*
Resolution: sublimation and release . . . *calmo e semplice*

A final note: it is interesting that "Jesus Christus unser Heiland," the most distressed of all the sixteen chorale settings in *Clavierübung,* book 3, seems so far in sentiment from the hymn it ostensibly glosses. The words of this Communion hymn are didactic, not affective. Only one of its seven stanzas has been offered, without too much conviction, as an incentive toward Dufourcq's "tormented chromaticism": stanza 2, paraphrasing Jesus' words in the Gospel of St. Matthew about the bread and wine—"take, eat, this is my body" and "this is my blood of the New Testament."

But when Bach wrote his Passion According to St. Matthew,

it was typically the torment of the soul that incited distress, in arias such as "Buß und Reu" and "Erbarme dich," not the Eucharist. He greeted the Last Supper with confidence and a special, simple beauty, in the bass arioso "Nehmet, esset; das ist mein Leib."

Fugue in F-sharp Minor

The Well-Tempered Clavier, Book 1

This fugue stands out among Bach's more celebrated *affettuoso* fugues in F-sharp minor and related keys, such as the imposing Fugue in B Minor later in *The Well-Tempered Clavier* and both Kyries from the Mass in B Minor, for its immediacy as well as its brevity. The countersubject with its ceaselessly sobbing figure has reminded many—indeed, most—commentators of the chorus "O Mensch bewein' dein' Sünde groß" from the St. Matthew Passion, and the chromatically tinged subject too practically cries out for words, words in the affective poetic language of Bach's cantata librettists Salomo Franck, Marianne von Ziegler, or Picander. The inching upward and falling back of the melodic line could paint the Christian soul in the toils of sin, or Christ Himself bearing the cross.

Was there ever a moment when this subject matter couldn't make up its mind whether it wanted to be a fugue or a da capo aria in some anguished cantata? For this "beautiful and haunting work," as Laurence Dreyfus calls it, also troubles him, as it has others, on account of anomalous or at least unusual features.

The pathos comes very largely—though not exclusively, as I hope I can show—from the powerful affect of the basic material; the sobbing of the countersubject persists even when the subject is inverted. Apart from this inversion, the fugue makes use of no fugal device or artifice. A beautiful stretto that starts in bar 22 fades almost immediately (and a possible exact inversion of the countersubject is never actuated).

The music does not modulate, except to the obligatory dominant key, C-sharp minor—an unusual if not an isolated circumstance for this composer. The mediant, A major, which one would also think obligatory, is just barely acknowledged *[bar 15];* major-mode sonorities are in very short supply. This makes for a profound austerity, to which a few short episodes, using mostly the same material, offer a little mitigation, even though that material derives, as usual, from the subject. It is as though having invented the most emotion-drenched subject/countersubject unit he could, Bach wanted to see if he could sustain a fugue with nothing else.

Not quite nothing else: if he draws very little on contrapuntal resources, he manipulates texture as a way of shaping the musical discourse. A distinct textural change divides the composition in three. Trio texture, with a "walking" bass a good distance below only two upper top voices, distinguishes a middle section or middle phase of the piece occupying a higher range than the others *[bars 20–27].* It is demarcated on both sides by similar cadences in the dominant key, C-sharp minor.

First Phase: *Bars 1–20*

The opening exposition takes up almost half of this fugue; we should track it closely.

- *Bars 1–7:* The basic material seems especially painful because it moves haltingly; the unexpected pause on note 3 makes the following three-note figure falter or stumble. (The long note 3 receives royal treatment later.) Then the subject simply stops, leaving the space between subject and answer unmediated: a strangely sedative gesture, again very unusual in terms of fugal practice.

  The countersubject, beginning with what amounts to a broken inversion of the subject—a forecast of the strict inversion that will materialize, and a hint of the stretto that will not—proceeds with a scale extending the subject's most decided move, eighth notes curling up through a fourth to the peak note C♯; the scale goes up to D♯. Another fourth, not a scale but a slower leap near the cadence, works to balance the continual stepwise motion.

  The first episode, fleeting as it may be, ventures up into a pitch region that has previously been denied to this constrained subject. It reaches the pitch B—a small message of consolation or hope, perhaps. If so it is dashed by the sobbing motif that takes over and drifts down, and down, into the third entry.

- *Bars 8–11:* The third entry develops a second countersubject, at first subsidiary, yet strong enough to surge over the other voices *[bar 10]*; it surges even more richly the next time *[18]*. The second episode starts with the same upward-curling figure as the first, but now without the sense of upward liberation. We do not even reach B this time, and C♯ is still some way in the future. We have to wait a considerable time for the next entry.

- *Bars 12–18:* This appears on the tonic, rather than on the dominant as anticipated, and as Roger Bullivant observes, given the long delay it sounds less like the completion of a four-part exposition than a new departure—a new exposition, with an extra voice added to the three we already know about. (We were not necessarily expecting a fourth voice, after all. The Prelude is for three.) Perhaps Bach chose the tonic to avoid invading the space above high C♯, where the more usual dominant entry would have taken him, and to allow the subject to stand out, in the soprano, yet also stay low, so as to set off the central trio section, which lies conspicuously higher. Besides the delay and the texture, this entry owes its climactic effect to the range—low as it is, it touches the highest pitches heard so far—and to rich doublings of fragments from both countersubjects, at the tenth and the sixth. The end of the second countersubject guides in the low cadence *[bar 18]*.

Second Phase: *Bars 20–28*

There is a sense of release as the soprano moves even higher and the texture thins and widens, leading to a more decisive cadence in bar 20. The subject appears again, in inversion—an inversion the composer appears to have obscured deliberately, by means of a faster, more articulate line above it. At all events it is easy to miss.

In the soprano entry (recto) that comes next, the walking bass of the trio texture unwinds to provide an interesting, almost bright new perspective on the fugal material *[bars 26–28]*. Bach obscures the opening of this recto statement too, this time melodically rather than contrapuntally.

Third Phase: *Bars 28–40*

Phase 1 of the fugue moved to an expressive climax in its last, four-part entry. Broadly recapitulatory in quality, phase 3 resumes this process, building up to a level of pathos—we can indeed speak of passion—well in excess of the promise even of this fugue's highly charged subject matter.

On the matter of sectionalization: admittedly, the break between what I am calling phases 2 and 3 of the Fugue in F-sharp Minor is fuzzier than that between 1 and 2. Busoni, for one, heard the work as a two-part structure and railed against the

idea of a three-part division. My phase 3, with its first subject
entry still in three voices, and with the soprano still in the same
high range as in the trio—even higher, one could say—can seem
like a continuation of phase 2. However, that subject entry (in the
tenor) returns to the tonic, after clear cadential articulation *[bar
28]*. Phase 1 of the fugue has three of its four entries starting on
the tonic, both entries of phase 2 start on the dominant, and
phase 3 has all three of its entries on the tonic.

Leaps of a fourth emerge around the tenor entry of bars 29–
32 and multiply around the bass entry that follows directly—
another inverted entry, now in four parts, and still in the tonic
[bars 32–35]. This inversion no one will miss; an outer voice, the
bass, tenders the subject unequivocally. (Was the earlier inverted
entry muted so that this one would speak more eloquently?
Whereas in the recto subject a single harmony underpins notes
1–3, in the inversion that critical note 3 acquires an affective
new harmony.) It is a moment of high pathos, with the bass
tracking the beginning of the soprano's winding descent to the
final cadence.

An inverted "answer" on the tonic—that certainly breaks textbook rules for a fugal answer. Yet this indeed feels like an answer
in a nontechnical sense, a subdued but entirely alert response to
the recto, a response that deepens dialogue. Hugo Riemann spoke
of "a greater inwardness, a deeper sinking into self."

Bach has raised the emotional stakes here and still holds a
king and an ace at the ready. More fourth leaps lead into a particularly plangent circle-of-fifths sequence, gleaming with major-
mode sonorities *[bars 35–36]*. The sobbing of the softly touching
lines is relieved by the doubling in tenths and sixths; this resource
was employed before, as we have seen, but never so expressively.

There is a special poignancy to major-mode chords—B, E, A, and D major, never presented quite explicitly—in a work that has rationed them until now. As this final episode ends—after only two and a half bars, though its shadow haunts bars 37–40—its offer of alleviation is trumped by an extraordinary augmented chord C♯ E♯ A♮ in the final subject entry. This chord reharmonizes note 3 once again, now over a dominant pedal *[bar 37]*. Dissonant, wrenching moments are not all that rare near the ends of Bach pieces, but this one bites harder than most.

By bringing the subject at the same pitch level, the final entry recapitulates the exposition's fourth entry. More broadly, the three tonic entries in bars 28–40 recapitulate the entire tonic-weighted exposition, bars 1–20. The final *tierce de Picardie* is one of Bach's most beautiful.

So I do not agree with Laurence Dreyfus that this fugue "seems to suggest a relatively static rather than dynamic reading," and that for Bach

> it was the number and quality of inventions that he could coax from his materials rather than their exhibited sequence that counted. For this reason, it is more compelling to hear the piece as a logical succession of paradigmatic changes rather than syntagmatic causalities: chains of metaphors rather than metonymies, as it were.

Indeed I find it hard to distinguish my clear sense of the sequence exhibited in this piece from its emotional immediacy. Baroque composers depict the passions, Romantic composers express them—this was a fairly common formulation before the concept of expression had taken a beating from recent aesthetic philosophers. Expression is more likely to be located now in the listener's ear rather than in the composer's pen, let alone his heart. So be it—for this listener there is an unmediated quality to this music, an intimation of the personal and the private that is unusual in Baroque music. The material itself has much to do with this quality but so also does the way the material is deployed in time.

In both Kyries of the B-Minor Mass, communal passion, communal pathos is distanced—as is of course entirely appropriate—and in the B-Minor Fugue from *The Well-Tempered Clavier,* book 1, what seems like personal pathos is theatricalized. These are grand, elaborate compositions, far overshadowing the terse, almost minimal Fugue in F-sharp Minor. That very terseness empowers special expressive immediacy.

CHAPTER 12

Gigue

English Suite no. 3 in G Minor

The characteristic Bach gigue can be considered (that is, heard) as a special type of fugue in a strictly prescribed, hypersymmetrical binary form—hypersymmetrical because these fugues come to a dead stop in the middle, allowing for an exact repetition of each of the two sections, or strains. Such gigues make very satisfying endings for about half of Bach's keyboard suites, the English Suites, the French Suites, and the Partitas, which also include some terminal gigues of a different, nonfugal type.

All but one of the fugal gigues are written for three voices, though they often use the full texture for the subject entries and drop the third voice soon afterward. These are dance-music pieces, the last and fastest members of the suites they belong to—too fast to allow for much maneuvering with three contrapuntal voices. Even in works that keep the texture full throughout, the counterpoint is usually just a tad informal.

As to harmony, modulation is not a resource much drawn on, presumably because binary form imposes its own tonic-to-dominant-to-tonic axis so monolithically. As a rule these fugues present entries in no more than three different keys, only occasionally four.

First Strain: *Bars 1–20*

The subject of the Gigue from English Suite no. 3 stands out for its élan, even among the high-spirited company of gigues in Bach's suites and those of his contemporaries. Its free fall through the interval of a twelfth is broken by sudden jerks, making for a humorous ending at a point where many fugue subjects lapse into convention.

The episodes are particularly imaginative in this gigue—past a couple of less than remarkable ones at the start *[bars 5–6, 8–11]*. The heavy half cadence after episode 2 bisects the first strain of the gigue, stressing the overall symmetry and highlighting the one mid-strain subject entry *[bars 12–13]*. Episode 3 is a composite lasting for five bars (that is, for a quarter of the strain). Its first, sequential segment *[bars 13–15]* introduces a cross-rhythm that knocks the strong beat from note 1 of the $\frac{12}{8}$ bars to note 7. Thus the episode's second segment—built on a powerfully measured upward scale from low A in the left hand—comes in a displaced meter, which the rhythmicized step up from C♯ to D in the left hand confirms with an irresistible swing *[bar 17]*. The point of this new metrical arrangement is to reverse accents in the subject when Bach retrieves it for use at the central cadence, where it reaches the dominant key in the middle of bar 20, making this an effective downbeat. The effect is paradoxical—less like a witticism, perhaps, than a conjuring trick.

A common, almost a defining feature of pieces in binary form is the use of a highly characteristic cadential phrase for each of their strains, to hammer home the binary symmetry. (*The Well-Tempered Clavier* exemplifies this in a dozen preludes and even one fugue, B-flat Major in book 2: see page 126.) Bach sometimes generates these cadential phrases out of the opening material, modified in some interesting way. Here the opening subject returns at the end of strain 1 newly invigorated, by means of note-against-note two-part counterpoint, and it performs its cadence on the newly established downbeat with the greatest of aplomb. There is a smell of burning rubber when the music stops.

Second Strain: *Bars 21–44*

The second strain of the G Minor Gigue tracks the first closely. (The main differences are the lack of a central half cadence and the presence of two mid-strain subject entries rather than one.) As in nearly all gigues, the second strain presents the subject in inversion, and as is often the case, this causes just a little awkwardness in the melody, for when the inverted subject curls down to the third degree (B♭) in bar 22 it wants to keep moving down, not up to C. Bach does not shirk the problem but fixes it by modifying the subject so that it sails up to the fifth degree (G, in a subdominant entry) *[bars 32–33]*. The modified subject initiates a relatively spacious, even grand descent in episode 6 *[33–34]*. While this may be a hectic piece, it does have its checks and balances.

We can expect some of the episodes in strain 2 of the gigue to recapitulate matter from strain 1, transposed down a fifth, but the smaller episodes are new. Only the corresponding composite episode 7 *[bars 36–41]* looks back to episode 3. Bypassing the disruptive beginning segment with the cross-accents, it extends that highly kinetic upward scale in the left hand beyond belief. The original parade of quarter notes, A B I C♯ - - - D E I F G (A), now gets extra cohorts: G ↘I E F♯ G A I B♭ C marching up into D E I F♯ - - - G A I B♭ C D.

This unbelievably long climb has upset some listeners but exhilarated others, who hear it as a spectacular augmentation of the inverted subject, appreciate the interesting countermotion in the right hand, and find the hyperbolic linear energy a perfect match for the explosive contrapuntal energy in the gigue's concluding salvo. For what now ensues is unusually brilliant, even by Bach's standards. When the subject (still inverted) turns up again to make the final cadence, it kicks off a new double stretto—with the original recto version of the subject *[bars 41–43]*. The recto entries are smartly tailored and unhampered by extra counterpoints. The afterbeat to the cadence clicks in punctually as a token of symmetry between the strains, but this has been symmetry with a difference.

(The idea of having the recto return in the second strain of a gigue to invade the inversion's space and effect a sort of recapitulation—this plays out in one or two other Bach examples. Bach prepares for the return as early as episode 4 *[bars 25–26]*, an episode so tiny one would hardly distinguish it from the general swirl if not for its inclusion of the characteristic upward-sixth leap taken from the subject's recto version. By this time the episodes and everything else ought to be controlled by the inversion, not the recto, but the upward sixth picks up and distills what is no doubt the most distinctive feature of the recto subject, its humorous ending. Then in episode 5, when a small turning figure slips down no fewer than nine steps in sequence, and bathos threatens, the presence of the sixth leap turns bathos into high comedy *[bars 30–32]*. The sixth-leap figure also starts off episode 7 *[36–37]*.)

All this analysis: yet this is a fugue for performance and display, not a fugue for contemplation or study. As the culmination of English Suite no. 3—a suite that counts among its movements a brilliant concerto paraphrase calling for a two-manual harpsichord, a saraband with extravagant ornamentation, and a favorite gavotte that would steal the show if left to its own resources—this gigue has to dazzle and impress. Dance is of the essence here: jig, saltarello, tarantella, not counterpoint. Its hyperbinary form is arguably even more conducive to easy listening than that of the other dances of the suite that precede it. It features the eighteenth-century equivalent of a conga line.

Bach can have it both ways.

CHAPTER 13

Fugue in A-flat Major

The Well-Tempered Clavier, Book 1

This fugue, among the more concise pieces in *The Well-Tempered Clavier,* is much loved by players and admired in the literature, though what seem to be its special, perhaps unique, features have not been remarked on or discussed. One of these is the way the answer in this fugue tends to cleave to the subject. As the piece proceeds, one feels more and more that its basic material has to be the subject together with its answer, which may be called the "subject-pair"—the subject-pair, not the single subject. The linkage is a consequence of the "open" ending of the subject, on the fifth degree, E♭, rather than on the more stable and much more common third degree or tonic, and of its rhythmic profile: entirely even, up to the point where it is firmly end-stopped.

Bach is articulating an elemental, elementary rhythmic cliché:

Twinkle, twinkle, little star,
How I wonder what you are,

one *and* two *and* three *and* FOUR—one *and* two *and* three *and* FOUR. True, the melodic contour of the subject ensures that it doesn't feel quite as jejune as that, only very simple. The wonder is how in so short a time so much eloquence can be made to emerge from such childlike beginnings. While the subject-pairs may be rudimentary and identical in rhythm, they are not identical or altogether simple in pitch content. The pitch configuration is modified so as to register distress *[bars 17–19]* or convey different shades of quiet enthusiasm and release *[23–25, 29–31]* or touch on real sorrow *[27–29]*.

Emotional range is another special feature of this short composition, all the more remarkable because of the overall tone of restraint.

First Phase: *Bars 1–23*

The flowing sixteenth-note figures of this fugue, which contrast with the more slowly flowing subject, are worth some close attention. They come in many slightly different patterns, culminating in the bass of the recurring episode first heard in bars 11–13. At their first appearance in bars 2–3 these figures do not shape themselves into a countersubject but propel the end of the answer into a slightly awkward sequence: Eb↗Ab G Eb↗ C Ab | Bb ∫ Eb↗Bb G Eb↗Ab F | G. This is the one place in the fugue where the subject-pair does not end-stop.

One would never guess the role destined for the pattern of sixteenths below the third entry, in the bass *[bars 5–6]*—until Bach repeats it several more times in an episode, as though to establish its bona fides as a latter-day countersubject *[7–9]*. It will track the subject at bar 18 (in inversion) and then in bars 23, 24, and 29.

After this repetitive, almost ruminative episode come three parallel segments, each presenting a subject entry or subject-pair leading to a new recurring episode, a filled-out version of the sequence adumbrated in bar 3 *[bars 10–13, 13–15, 17–20]*. The awkwardness has disappeared. The triple counterpoint appears each time in different contrapuntal inversions, and one could hardly find a better instance to illustrate the expressive power of this device. Hugo Riemann observed that these episodes do not feel like "independent, real 'between' members in the period structure," as is generally the case in fugues, but like essential completions or fulfillments (*Vollziehungen*) of the entries themselves. Tovey went so far as to declare the episodes, not the subject entries, the most important events in this composition.

At least to some extent, these responses must be due to the episode's intrinsic beauty. Although utterly simple in harmony— it moves around the circle of fifths with the usual standard suspensions—the detailing is exquisite: the flickers of dissonance caused by *échappée* notes such as the C at the end of bar 11, and the momentary lift caused by the pair of sixteenth notes in bar 20.

The entries that are "fulfilled" by this recurring episode come first on the tonic, then on the submediant (F minor), and then on the supertonic (B-flat minor, answered by another entry confirming that key). This is the area in the fugue that modulates, then, introducing minor-mode sonorities made sumptuous by the four-part writing. A strong cadence in the dominant, E flat major, is guided in by the suggestion of another entry, in the alto, with a feint at stretto in the soprano *[bars 21–23]*. It is more than a suggestion; one can hear the whole subject, extended so as to reach a firm close, as though the notation were as shown in example 17. Compare bars 33–35; the Fugue in A-flat is actually a camouflaged member of the family of fugal compositions evoking the binary structure of dance form. We have met or will

Example 17

22

meet several of these family members: the Fughetta in C, BWV 952, the G-Minor Gigue, and the Fugue in B-flat Major from book 2 of the *WTC*.

Second Phase: *Bars 23–35*

After this strong, form-defining cadence, the fugue opens up onto a serene, drawn-out plateau, a sort of diffused and moderated area of climax. Again, this is a feature that seems special to this composition.

The new subject-pairs flow into new episodes, just as brief as the previous recurring episode and just as articulate and integral. In bars 23–25 the subject itself changes in two seemingly contradictory ways. Melodically it expands, as the interval of a sixth (the key interval that furnished the melody with its peak) stretches to a seventh, while harmonically it contracts, since the melodic change allows a single dominant-seventh chord to underpin every beat until the last. Contrapunctus 4 in *The Art of Fugue* includes a memorable similar case, though in that case the thematic expansion of a sixth to a seventh promotes a dramatic intensification of harmony. In the Fugue in A-flat the subject-pair does not register drama at this point but liberation, new lyricism, and grace. David Ledbetter calls the subject of this fugue "lovable"; it is never more lovable than here.

The next fulfilling episode resembles the previous ones in some ways, but unlike them, it cannot be imagined in contrapuntal inversion, with the original soprano line half-hidden away in the lower voices. This episode celebrates melody, escalating melody, almost "unending melody" in Wagner's sense. It eases the melodic line downward from the expansive soprano entry in bar 24 with wonderfully mellow arabesques and then goes on to initiate another, second linear descent, over the next entries *[bars 27–30]*.

The last two subject-pairs join to form a full, and therefore quietly climactic exposition of the fugue's four voices. The steady pulsation works its way up ceremoniously and radiantly through the bass, tenor, alto, and soprano to join the overarching soprano melody. The soprano entry is the highest yet, and the arabesques, inverted, mount higher still, outdoing themselves in eloquence, then becoming a chain of descending thirds (A♭ F D♭ B♭ G): music for a benediction *[bar 32]*. When the soprano moves down again the childlike rhythm breaks:

> Twinkle, twinkle, twinkle, little star
> You are.

The upper voices have been coalescing into rather grand chords. At the very end the flowing sixteenth notes in the bass shape themselves into a distinctive figure—the expressive figure from the recurring episode, the figure with the dissonant *échappée* *[bars 34, 35]*. The fugue ends by "rhyming" with its central cadence, enhanced by this new reminiscence, spoken in an undertone: restrained, like all the rest of the music, but telling.

From the diaries of Cosima Wagner we know that late in his life Richard Wagner admired Bach and especially *The Well-Tempered Clavier.* "The quintessence of Bach," he called it, comparing the fugues to "the roots of words . . . in relation to other music it is like Sanskrit to other languages."

One winter a fabulous series of soirées at Haus Wahnfried, the Wagner mansion in Bayreuth, was given over to the whole of the *WTC,* six preludes and fugues per evening, with Josef Rubinstein and Liszt playing and Wagner holding forth. "R. describes the 17th fugue [A-flat Major] as a dance, and traces a few steps to the first bars, then says it is freer in form, already approaching the sonata," Cosima writes. This seems a little off for our fugue— Cosima may have confused the number. But another of her comments, "R. cannot praise highly enough the remarkable singing quality of the figurations," referring to the *WTC* in general, might have been prompted by the sixteenth-note figures of the Fugue in A-flat Major.

(Wagner specifically related his "unending melody" to another *WTC* fugue, the Fugue in F-sharp Minor from book 2. An essay by Christian Thorau discusses the aptness of this choice at length.)

CHAPTER 14

Fugue in A Minor

Fantasy and Fugue in A Minor, BWV 904

Where to start is with two pages at the center of the Fugue in A Minor—the essential pages, containing a second, free fugue within the three-part sectional form (A B A'). In section 3 of the work, A', new themes developed in section 2 will combine with the subject of section 1.

This central fugue circulates a familiar-sounding chromatic subject twice through each of the four voices. This seems a better way of describing the overall plan than to speak of two (irregular) four-part expositions, for the entries all come in pairs—with substantial and specially important episodes between them; the motif of the first of these episodes is worked into a freely varied countersubject. And the time interval between entries expands from two beats in the first pair of entries, which therefore counts as a close stretto between bass and alto *[bars 37–39]*, to four beats—one bar—in the second pair *[41–44]*, a bar and a half in the third *[48–51]*, and two bars in the fourth and last *[55–59]*.

Clearly this music's almost surplus expressivity has not been achieved at the expense of systematic thinking. Bach does not employ system for system's sake, however, at least not here. The result of the time interval's expanding (or, looked at another way, the stretto's unwinding) is that we get a bigger allotment of descending semitones each time. They soon become hypnotic.

The episodes are specially important because of the essentially neutral affect of the main, chromatic theme itself (which I am happier calling "theme," rather than "subject"; it lacks the cogency of a typical Bach subject, even though it can serve as such in a subsidiary capacity). Anyone's instinctive response to this pattern of slow descending semitones will probably be to lament along with them, as we do with Dido's Lament in Purcell's *Dido and Aeneas,* the Crucifixus in Bach's Mass in B Minor, and any number of other unforgettable moments in opera, church music, and the repertory of organ chorales.

But in fact this chromatic pattern also turns up again and again in Baroque music not associated with any text, so much so that it counts as one of the era's insistent clichés. The Bach scholar Peter Williams, who has written a whole book on the history of *The Chromatic Fourth,* from Cipriano de Rore and William Byrd to Bartók and Stravinsky, cites its appearance in about fifty instrumental works by Bach. (And he must have chosen his examples from among many more, since the Fantasy and Fugue in A Minor is not among them.) Whether composers meant to evoke the affect of lament in the many instrumental fugues that use the chromatic fourth as a subject, countersubject, or subsidiary subject, is a real question. Williams thinks not.

Some of these fugues are certainly quite dry. However, the

accents of lament must always be at least *latent* in the chromatic subjects, always open to the possibility of activation by means of some further musical parameter or device. Here this function is filled by the one-bar motif introduced in the first episode *[bar 39]*. Its anapest rhythm and its syncopation survive through an almost unthinkable diversity of variations, the variants becoming more and more expressive and even more hypnotic than the descending semitones.

This music lives on its wealth of exquisite detail, for which no level of sensitivity can be too hyper. At the keyboard one follows it fascinated—in my case, I have to say, with a keyed-up mixture of feelings like delight, admiration, and apprehension. Things are harder at the word processor, frequent raids on the thesaurus key ALT–FI notwithstanding. With music of this kind we really have to go bar by bar, beat by fascinating beat.

Fugue 2: *Bars 36–60*

The new fugue begins directly after the final entry of the original subject *[bars 33–36]*, the subject of fugue 1 (fugue 1 is discussed below).

· *Bars 36–38:* The rhythmic transition here is very striking. When the sixteenth-note motion tapers off into quarters (articulated as a heavy staccato) there is a feeling of uncertainty that deepens with the slack appoggiatura D–C (not D–C♯) in the alto. The cadence seems unsure of its own finality, as though sensing something untoward ahead in the stretto's tread of unvarying quarter notes. There are as many as nine of these quarters in all.

· *Bars 39–41:* The pace has to pick up again, and when it does the rhythm of the all-important new motif too is uncertain, or at least halting (see example 18a). As the motif begins to probe chro-

Example 18

matic space, we can also hear it as vulnerable and wary. The peak note of its anapest figure is nearly always hit by a dissonance caused by the surrounding counterpoint (at its first appearance, D♯ in the alto makes a dissonance with C in the bass). Often, as here, the dissonance or its impression lingers on, delaying its resolution until the last moment.

- *Bars 41–43:* Manipulating the motif into a countersubject to the chromatic theme becomes a very delicate procedure. Bach first tests the waters with just the motif's ending figure. He adds the rest of it almost covertly, on a weak beat (example 18b), though the material gains confidence (and credibility as a countersubject) inasmuch as the motif now appears as a sequence drawn out as a melodic line in a single voice, rather than shared between imitating voices.

- *Bar 43:* A new arpeggio figure eases the motif over onto the strong beat; as happens almost routinely in this music, one idea flows into another seamlessly and with the greatest eloquence (example 18c).

- *Bars 44–47:* Fugue 2 is laid out symmetrically or systematically, at least for a while, with episodes of the same sort after the first and second pairs of entries (though the latter is in three parts and is extended) *[bars 41–43, 44–47].* If the motif seemed (to me) fearful before, now its worst fears have been realized and it settles into varieties of plaint or lament. This affective posture matches the aptitude of the chromatic theme only too well.

  Again the motif gains coherence when its sequences run together in a single voice, and urgency as well, for the voice is the soprano and this has moved up rather suddenly to high C. The descent is slow.

- *Bar 47:* Bach also plays with the eighth-note figure from the episodes, drawing a burst of emotion from it in a truly vertiginous transformation (example 18d). One can hear this cry in the tenor as an anticipation of a whole series of such transformations coming up in the soprano.

- *Bars 48–50:* Few bars in the whole of this work depart from the minor mode—only two bars in fugue 1 and two in fugue 2. The present entries in C and G major cloud major modality with minor-mode nuance and ambivalent dissonances.

  Above these entries the variants of the motif sound to me more than plaintive, they sound excruciating; the sixteenth-note anapest figure originally heard as *step ↗ step ↗* (A–B–C), treated to some kind of out-of-control inversion process, shatters into

more extreme figures: first *diminished 5th↘ step↗*, then its dis-
torting-mirror image *diminished 5th↗ step↘, minor 6th↘ step↗*,
and finally a piercing *minor 7th↘ step↗* (example 18e).

- *Bars 51–53:* This very fraught passage needs relief and gets it,
from a fresh episode using the basic material in mild ways (example 18f). There are still descending semitones in the upper voices
but never two in a row, and the version of the motif low down in
the bass feels open and kinetic. After a few leaps and bounds this
version converts back into the original motif, at its original register—another seamless, eloquent transition (example 18g).

- *Bars 53–54:* Once back to its natural habitat in the alto-soprano
range, the motif is ready to mutate again. A simple, soft variant
slips down—by this time we are listening to every heartbeat—
into a beautifully molded half cadence (example 18h) and then
slips up again, in a sort of pensive rebound (example 18i). The
soprano waits for the alto to join it on the note B (example 18j).
The alto itself waits for another lingering resolution. The music
is waiting for the final pair of entries, a tenor-soprano pair that
will form the climax to this section of the fugue.

- *Bars 54–59:* This climax employs another expressive variant of
the motif, which in the first entry of the pair comes at the interval of an *augmented fourth* above the chromatic theme, on the
weak beat (example 18k), and in the second entry a *major sixth*
below it, on the *strong* beat (example 18l).

  Ever-new wrenching dissonances are the outcome of this
technical tour de force. Each of the two entries gets special
enhancement: the first of them is supported by the lowest pitches
so far, led into by a marvelous leap in the left hand down from
high to low E. The whole bass line pulses with new resonance.
The second entry draws on the full four-part texture for the first
time . . . and brings a (more or less) new rhythmic figure in the
tenor, expressive to the last . . .

- *Bars 59–60:* Can we really keep up with all this, and thrill to it?
Although the themes remain at work after what is really the
final cadence, in bar 56, they are now more transparent than
expressive. A "cleared-up" variant of the motif over a de facto

dominant pedal makes a perfectly paced transition back to fugue 1 (example 18m—a quite remote variant, though bar 53 offers a precedent). Bach writes a simple little stretto here, as a farewell to a motif in the process of (temporary) liquidation.

The dissonances are still there, defanged. The chromatic fourth withdraws to the emotional neutrality that Peter Williams says is its normal condition in instrumental writing of the Baroque.

Fugue 1: *Bars 1–36*

Sir Hubert Parry called the Fugue in A Minor "one of Bach's very finest fugues"—and has been criticized for it. (Parry wrote one of three major studies of the composer that came out almost at the same time, in 1905–9, the first of any consequence since Philipp Spitta's foundational study of thirty years earlier. The others were by Albert Schweitzer and the French musicologist André Pirro.) Of course I agree with Parry.

But even Parry would not have called this music *consistently* very fine. The awkwardness of the first subject comes into focus if it is compared to a sample from *The Well-Tempered Clavier* similar to it in contour (see example 19): too many heavy beats, too many As and Ds, and the diminution in bar 7 is too obvious. The comparison makes one wonder, incidentally, how later authorities can rest easy with a date as late as 1725 for this music. They have built a good case that the Fugue in A Minor and the Fantasy—a superb extended essay in concerto form— were not written together as a pair and probably not brought together by the composer; whether the fugue's three sections in their present form were written together as late as 1725 has not been investigated.

Other weaknesses show up in section 1—as well as more fine

Example 19

a. Fugue in A Minor, BWV 904 (answer)

b. Fugue in F-sharp Minor, *WTC,* book 2 (answer, transposed)

things for Parry to admire, starting with the link between the opening entry and the answer. After the subject's prolix ending, any composer would probably want to move upward with some vigor, but to run (or race) its characteristic interval of a minor sixth up to the top of the keyboard and hang there—*that* could not have been predicted. This haunting sound never recurs.

The lack of a real countersubject allows for new harmonies at later entries, as well as varied counterpoints; bars 25–28 are particularly rich. An episode working through some major keys makes an energetic foil to the main material *[bars 29–32]*. It combines the end of the subject with parts of the link and returns expertly modified so as to fit the deepening sobriety—gloom, we may as well call it—that settles in on the fugue's last page *[bars 71–74]*.

This music is monolithic; fugue 1 might be picked out to exemplify the world of the Baroque, the world Bach knew in his early years, while fugue 2 looks forward to the music of sensibility, the *empfindsamer Stil* of a younger generation. Here the music is constantly evolving. Its emotion is nursed within; if fugue 2 laments, it does so alone in a private space, not communally at any kind of public ritual. Fugue 1 is severe, rhetorical, admonitory. The voice may be hoarse, but the lesson is momentous. One fugue suffers, the other sermonizes.

The Fugue Subjects Combined: *Bars 61–80*

In no other fugue of this type does Bach draw so extreme a contrast between sections (allowing for one equivocal exception: the unfinished Contrapunctus 14 in *The Art of Fugue*). How does he accommodate the contrasted worlds of section 1 and section 2 in section 3? Through melody and harmony, rather than counterpoint.

The combination of the three themes in triple counterpoint works less well than one might have expected—less well, at least, than I would have expected—for while the chromatic theme does its job dependably in the wake of the main subject, the expressive motif comes rather too late, and its initial launch in the high register does not bear comparison with similar launches earlier *[bars 63, 43 and 53]*. We also miss the tenor. But the motif reaches a kind of apogee over the last stretto of the chromatic theme, wedged in between entries of the main subject *[bars 67–68]*. The two upper voices go high, entwine, fuse, and implode into a de facto run of continuous sixteenth notes. The motif seems to yearn as it disappears in a new liquidation.

And the big moment in section 3 comes at the encounter of all the themes in the last of its three combined subject entries *[bars 74–78]*. (The second of the combined entries, in shock from the liquidation of the motif, leaves the motif out and uses only the other two themes.) Clearly this is the rhetorical climax of the whole composition. The original subject has been reharmonized before, as we have seen, but never as drastically as here—the forthright subdominant on the third beat of bar 74, the flicker of modal harmony in the C-major chord on the fourth beat, and its realization in the magnificent low C three bars later. Bach's homily comes through with unshakable authority.

Only after these moments have passed does the crucial motif come into play, with a gesture that reclaims the subtlety of its operations in fugue 2. It bonds quietly—so quietly that one hardly notices—with shreds of the main fugue subject on the way to the final cadence *[bars 78–80]*. A melodic invention of the simplest kind brings this fugue's two opposite emotional worlds into a final equilibrium.

CHAPTER 15

Fugue in B-flat Major

The Well-Tempered Clavier, Book 2

Writing on the Fugue in B-flat Major, Hermann Keller found the countersubjects "handled in an indolent, almost casual manner, in no way disturbing the serene unconcern of this fugue." These adjectives work rather well for the character of the piece in general, not only for the treatment of the countersubjects, though it's important to supplement them with another set of adjectives, adjectives like artful, elegant, and sly. Keller says that its performance should be "lightly animated, with grace and some humor." This work is one of Bach's more subtle inventions—a light-hearted fugue for connoisseurs, we should probably acknowledge, one that also labors under a further handicap, that of sharing space with one of the composer's most radiant (and longest) preludes.

Indolent: the lazy stream of sound begins with the fugue subject itself, a strictly continuous series of even notes in a moderate tempo. In slow tempo, a continuously moving subject can make a fugue sound grave and monumental (the Fugue in F Minor from

Example 20

The Well-Tempered Clavier, book 1), in fast tempo, brilliant (see example 2, page 18), and in moderate tempo, gently somnolent. The placid surface should not be allowed to hide the tough fugal structure below and its sophisticated contrapuntal manipulations.

Sly: while this subject is decidedly anomalous in opening on a pitch other than the tonic or the dominant—something that puts every commentator on alert—in this rhythmic situation one barely notices, so fluent is the motion. And of course the off-the-tonic, off-the-downbeat opening contributes to the fluency, a point particularly evident if one compares this fugal opening, on the supertonic, C, to the only other one in the *WTC* with a similar anomaly, F-sharp Major from book 2, with its zany trill on the hypersensitive seventh degree (example 20).

But most sly and artful of all is the phrase leading to the very strong cadence in the middle of this fugue—actually, not halfway through, more like a third *[bars 29–32]*. It is a phrase that seems to have migrated from another sound world, another era. More than one passage in the *WTC* shows Bach's interest in the music of sensibility, the *empfindsamer Stil* associated with his son Carl Philipp Emanuel, which grew up as a reaction to perceived severities of the Baroque. This is what Tovey had in mind when he spoke of a "homophonic crotchet bass" in this phrase and said it should be played "with the repeated notes nearly tied," so as to evoke the clavichord *Bebung* or vibrato effect favored by the younger generation.

Instead of flowing, the music here begins to slide, as though the only-too-well-established eighth-note motion were imperiled by the diminished fifth F↘(D)↘B♮ outlined by the bass *[bars 28–29]*, and the voice now needed to stabilize itself by means of steady quarter notes. Over this precarious-sounding foundation, the upper voices—suddenly aerated by rests—continue on their insouciant way, with a brisk little rhythmic snap in the soprano *[bar 31]*. The alto voice compounds the problem with its A♭ and then tries to put on the brakes with its long E♮. There are spicy harmonic details in bars 30 and 31: a progression from a diminished fifth to an augmented fourth (B–F / B♭–E) and a dissonant *échappée* note A.

No, what is *most* sly is how easily we find ourselves adjusting to the fugue's basic fluent style when the unsettling moment is past. We wonder whether we've been daydreaming. David Schulenberg suggests that the cadence "sounds a little pat, entering a bit too suddenly," but I think not. The effect has been anticipated, locally by the chromatic slippage in bars 26–27, and by the extraordinary dropping out of the upper voices in bar 28.

It has also been anticipated by broader rhythmic factors. With so fluent a gait, this music will either lull the listener into pleasant inattention or make her especially alert to the slightest rhythmic deviations. One call to attention is the syncopation followed by a pair of eighth notes in bar 8; Riemann noted that this figure blossoms in the fugue's longest episode, some sixty bars later—a reference that will give the specially alert listener special satisfaction. Another slight deviation is more immediate, the iambic pattern (quarter note/half note) introduced as a rhythmic contrast in the first episode. Bar 19 holds it in our memory, and it slows the movement in bars 25–27 and 28. Bar 31 offers a diminution, in that rhythmic snap. Artful again.

With so striking a central cadence, in the dominant, we know that the same striking cadence will return at the end of the work, transposed into the tonic. "Rhyming" cadences of this kind are a feature of binary compositions and fugues that borrow from them; see page 20.

Section 1: *Bars 1–32*

The structure of the subject allows for many subtleties. (Is it too sly to suggest that the two motifs in it, presented in different sorts of sequence, are making mild fun of standard Baroque figures for warfare and pathos, respectively?) Originally presented in the configuration *a a b b,* elsewhere the *a* and *b* motifs are reconfigured. The pattern *b a* seems especially piquant at the big cadences *[bars 29–30, 90–91].* The pattern *a b a b a b b* will add sinew to the fugue's longest episode *[69–75].*

And bar 9 introduces a slight variant of *a;* it would be fussy to distinguish this, if not for the fact that the inversion at the end of the variant usually points in some interesting direction: a leap of a fifth, echoing the new fifth in the answer *[bars 9, 11],* a downward seventh *[12, 45],* an unexpected A♭ *[14],* a sustained high F *[21].*

Section 1 of the fugue is short, simple, and notably lucid. A lot of space opens up between the bass and the upper voices. There are only four subject entries, and the countersubjects could not be simpler or more elegant. The one in the alto is little more than a long sustained note, and the one in the soprano consists of a long limping scale mirroring the *first* half of the subject while doubling the *second* half of the subject in tenths and sixths *[bars 13–17]*. These primitive countersubjects invert neatly to the soprano and alto respectively *[21–24]*.

Section 2: Bars 32–93

After the fugue's central cadence, combination of the subject with new, contrasting counterpoints articulates the beginning of a second section. They turn out to be true countersubjects, for although after their first appearance they tend to click in late—almost casually, as Keller put it—they persist quite audibly for many more entries and experience many more different inversions than do their opposite numbers in the fugue's first section.

(New—yet these countersubjects are also artfully linked to earlier material:

- The slow one, in the bass, augments the bass of the immediately preceding cadence *[bars 30–31, 32–36]*.
- The other draws its syncopation and two-eighth-note figure from bar 8. Its entire line, in fact, is foreshadowed in bars 6–9, and what might be viewed as the fully realized form of this countersubject opens with the half-inverted variant of the first motif from bar 9 *[40, 65]*.
- At one point in section 2, Bach winks at section 1, where the motif entered variously on the subject's first or second bar, by bringing it on both the first *and* the second bar of an entry *[14, 21, 54–55]*.)

The texture now becomes markedly denser. Contrapuntal inversions of the combined subject and countersubjects are worked out in unusually fertile and elegant ways. By the time of book 2 of the *WTC,* Bach was losing interest in those clearly

organized sequential episodes, designed to return in strict contrapuntal inversion, which play so large a role in book 1—starting
with the often-cited Fugue in C Minor. In the middle of the
present fugue, five separate subject entries are spaced out by transitional passages, none of which crystallizes out as a clearly
defined unit, ringing endless changes on the thematic material
[bars 32–67].

This is rich fare and, dare I say, somewhat hard to digest. The
invention is fabulous, and the saturation impressive. But as the
subject drifts smoothly and systematically through many keys—
from B-flat major to G minor, E-flat major, and C minor—I
think Keller is right to find something indolent in the regular
turnover of entries and spacing material, all at three-, four-, or
five-bar intervals—eight units, in all. I can sense a sort of gener-
alized purposefulness at this point in the composition; I miss an
overall sense of purpose.

However this may be, this dense music provides a foil for
Bach's next move: to bring the piece to an end with altogether
new expansiveness, and even a show of new power. The control
of pace here is as notable as the contrapuntal virtuosity in the previous bars. At this juncture Bach writes two longer phrases running into the "rhyming" cadence. The first of them contains an
episode that is very well calculated, simple as it may look on the
page *[bars 67–75]*: the sheer length of it, relative to the rest of the
fugue, the contented rumble of the bass, released from its
involved contrapuntal transactions, and the familiar, friendly
circle-of-fifths harmonic progression—all this leads firmly,
broadly, and with a certain formality to a moment of rest on the
dominant.

Then the fugue takes a gulp of air before launching into the final subject entry, an answer starting from high G *[bars 78–81]*. The sense of new breadth is maintained beautifully, as the subject is now drawn out for longer than four bars. This is not the first time Bach has created this effect with this subject, but it is especially striking on this occasion because the slow countersubject in the bass appears to slip out of synch and move ahead by one bar, thus refusing to close off the subject. The subject also refuses to close off itself, proliferating by means of a deliberate sequence to a cadence in G minor. (Though to be sure, as this was the key of the first entry to move away from the tonic-dominant sphere *[bars 47–51]*, one could say that *something* has been closed off, an area of modulation. G was the high note in bar 78.)

The creative energy seems limitless. In bar 86 the fugue's signature motif *a* turns upward, through the lively interval of a sixth, not downward as on all previous occasions. A single broken chord (see page 156) adds a moment of impulsive sparkle. (Or does the token swelling of the texture here, prior to the final cadence, "invert" the emptying of texture prior to the central cadence *[bars 88, 27–28]*? That would be sly.) From the high G at the beginning of the last entry on, the wide-open texture characteristic of the fugue's first section is restored and underscored.

A metaphor claims precedence, insists on its prerogatives, will not be hushed up. It figures our fugue as the outflow of a tiny spring, an indolent trickle in a single voice. The music swells into a stream, gathers volume, and flows merrily (that's the word) before being dammed for a moment; that funky central cadence behaves like a man-made barrier to the natural force of Baroque polyphony. A sluice, perhaps, or a lock. Past this, the waters enter into a stretch of tricky rapids, where they eddy and surge into adjacent tonal territory. Then the stream, now a rivulet, runs smoothly again, and in broader channels, opening upon what has become an ample vista . . . until another, rhyming sluice completely stems the flow and inundates the metaphor.

CHAPTER 16

Fugue in B Major

The Well-Tempered Clavier, Book 2

An entrée to the Fugue in B Major, one of Bach's most beautiful fugues, can be gained from a composer who learned *The Well-Tempered Clavier* as a boy and at the end of his life found himself drawing on it again and again. When Beethoven took the subject of the B Major Fugue as the model for that of the *Große Fuge,* the fugal finale of the Quartet no. 13 in B-flat Major, Opus 130, he turned Bach on his head. The upward corkscrew thrust of the *Große Fuge* subject generates an emphatic climax, driven home by a characteristic late-Beethoven trill (example 21).

Bach's aesthetic does not allow for a climax of this boisterous kind. Throughout the B Major Fugue one can see him working to tamp down excess energies inherent in the very unusual trajectory of his material. A melody that moves up an octave, from low tonic to high tonic, needs to recoup and find a safe resting place. The special quality of this work comes from a dialectic of aspiration and restraint, soaring upward and holding down.

Example 21

a. Beethoven, *Große Fuge*

b. Fugue in B Major, *Well-Tempered Clavier,* book 2

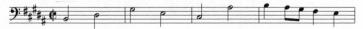

Thus in the opening exposition, the slow, measured tread of the subject reaches up to its climax just in time to break off and cede to a graceful tumble of shorter, weaker steps reclaiming the entire octave. In addition, as soon as possible—that is, after the first subject/answer pair—Bach softens the next pair harmonically, by underpinning their peak notes with submediants (G♯ under B in bar 13, D♯ under F♯ in bar 17). The successive notes of the subject, grouped as diads—B + D♯, E + G♯, A♯ + C♯— form themselves into the cadential progression I–IV–V–I; in bars 13 and 17 these cadences turn deceptive (I–IV–V–vi).

At this early point in the composition, Bach introduces the softening notes in such a way as to cause the mildest of interruptions to the suave harmonic flow—mild, though with a hint of ceremony, even austerity. A little later, in the fugue's second section, he brings the same subject/answer pair (same voices, same pitch levels) and undercuts the peaks with the same submediants *[bars 38, 45]*. Restraint of the climax now requires chromatic alterations and diminished-seventh sounds. These obviously foretell modulation. The different treatment of these submediants epitomizes the difference between the two sections of this fugue—the first ostensibly simple, the second obviously richer and much more fully developed.

Section 1: *Bars 1–27*

In its sectional form, the Fugue in B Major resembles the Fugue in B-flat Major, a few pages earlier in the *WTC,* at least at first blush, but the differences between them are revealing. In B-flat Major, after the central cadence two serious countersubjects are unleashed—adding up to three contrapuntal lines with just three voices to cope with them. B Major deals its subject two countersubjects in section 1 but only one in section 2, an easy enough hand for a composer with four voices at his disposal. No wonder (since the composer is Bach) the piece can flow in such effortless, stately periods.

He designed the intricate patterns of the first countersubject to offset the explicit rhythmic and implicit harmonic simplicities of the subject. It tracks the subject's risky upward course, twining around it like a vine, then untwining and descending in the closest conjunction with its sequel, so that the syncopations and dissonances all drop away. This quite marvelous two-part counterpoint casts a pensive gray light evenly over the opening page, as I hear it—*pace* Hugo Riemann, who admired the B-Major Fugue for its contrasts, for the subject's "steps of iron fate" and the countersubject's "passionate wringing of hands." However this may be or may be felt, the first section of this fugue certainly counts for a good deal more than a launching pad for the second.

Yet section 1 of the B-Major Fugue bests B-flat Major for simplicity, with barely perceptible links between entries, rather than episodes. (Note how smoothly Bach overlaps linking and episodic material with the upcoming entries, here and elsewhere.) After the exposition the countersubject breaks free at last and rises serenely to high G♯, the highest pitch yet *[bar 21]*. Two bars later G♯ is touched again—as though to remind us of the sensitivity of this note within the original subject. Entry 5 opens into a brief, relaxed passage preparing for the first big cadence, where a new figure appears in the lower voices—a softly-moving slow trill *[bars 22, 23, 24]*. It is rather distinctive, and we will not miss it when it returns.

Section 2: *Bars 27–60*

How fresh section 2 sounds; a gust of air blows through the texture as it starts, and the new countersubject (or second subject) could not contrast with the first more elegantly: flowing rather than spurting, headed down, not up, wide open, not entwined. Introduced along with the main subject, it is in fact the typical continuously moving member of Bach's contrapuntal combinations, if more shapely than most because of its contour and the syncopated braking at the end. Syncopation ties it in with the first countersubject, which it now completely displaces—lest there be any mistake about this, the next few bars busy themselves with a mini-exposition for the second subject all on its own.

This leads to an extended passage devoted to various thematic combinations and modulations. The strong tonic peaks tend to be softened, as we have seen; the submediant ploy makes for fluidity and ease in modulation. Except for the way it ends, this passage resembles the corresponding passage (directly after the central cadence) in the Fugue in B-flat Major, but things feel more lucid here, due mainly, no doubt, to the distinction in material between the episodes and the entries. All episodes (except the last) employ the same idea, as in section 1, but here it is a subsidiary idea: an almost routine scale figure gliding up and down the interval of a fourth in eighth notes. This figure can perhaps be traced back to bars 22–24 (or even to bar 4), and it stays with the piece until the final cadence.

One entry stands out because the subject's peak note is *not* softened by undercutting of its tonic. Entry 9, in G-sharp minor, proclaims its submediant tonality *[bars 48–51]*. Entry 11 will proclaim submediant authority. After visiting the submediant key twice we can hardly be surprised that this fugue will be even more extensive, intricate, and magnificent than at first we would have anticipated.

Bars 60–85

Hearty, almost Handelian right-hand chords prepare the important E-major cadence in bar 60. They may already warn of bumps ahead in what has been a very smooth ride up to now.

Entry 11 suddenly claims a higher register, and a higher adrenaline level: the soprano bursts in at the top of its range with the countersubject a bar ahead of time (triggered by a flashback in the alto to the syncopations of the earlier countersubject: bars 60–64). The subject itself starts *in* E major but *on* G♯, so that it ends in the submediant, for the second time, as already noted. Now there is space for a substantial episode, at long last, moving down, up—high up—and down again in three distinct segments *[bars 63–74]*. With a growing sense of exhilaration and release, sixteenth notes and leaping dotted figures renew the aspiration inherent in the original subject.

Entry 12 *[bars 75–78]:* one can see why commentators refer to a climax at this juncture—Schulenberg even speaks of a "sonata-style return"—for both the tonic key and the four-part texture are

Example 22

restored, after a long absence (example 22). Yet again there is a sense of restraint; this return is nothing like a Beethoven recapitulation. The tonic at bar 75 is prepared very weakly, and the commanding soprano line picks out notes of the submediant triad, once again (D♯, B, G♯, D♯), rather than those of the tonic. The energy generated by those submediant proclamations seems still not to have dissipated. In fact G♯ receives its strongest articulation yet within this very entry, appearing first in the bass with the luminous support of a secondary dominant, a D-sharp-major chord *[bars 75–76],* and then at the top of the soprano melody *[77].*

And G sharp seems still strong enough to deflect the harmony back to its cohort, the mediant D-sharp minor, site of the next strong cadence *[bar 85].* In a strange way the tonic area of entry 12 feels like a parenthesis between the keys of G-sharp minor and D-sharp minor to come, a major-mode area trapped between two minor-mode ones. It is hard enough to describe what happens here in technical terms, let alone characterize the feeling: stable and unstable, warm and distant, new and old—old, since entry 12 resonates with another bass entry in the tonic, entry 5, from the end of section 1 *[bars 19–21].* The gliding scale figure that was broached there emerges from the shadows for a gesture of unexpected eloquence *[bars 77–78].*

Bars 85–104

The cadence in D-sharp minor balances the previous cadence in E major *[bar 60]* in solidity and also in function—though not in texture: like the upcoming entry and episode, it is in three parts only. The function is to set up a deceptive staging area for a new entry. Just as E major masked a launch from G♯, the submediant, D-sharp minor masks a launch from F♯, the dominant; and the function of the dominant entry is to stabilize the final tonic entry. The short trio episode that comes in between *[bars 89–92]* might be thought too naive for a place in this composition, just as the earlier long episode might be thought too rhapsodic, but Bach knits both styles seamlessly and beautifully into a continuum.

The saga of the submediants ends in entry 14 *[bar 93]*, the final tonic entry, which, unlike the previous tonic entry, entry 12, has been fully prepared. (That was the simple function of the simple episode.) G♯ still underpins bar 1 of the subject, as well as resonating subtly in bar 2. But the coloration is now not submediant but subdominant; the E-major harmony implied in the original subject (bar 2) comes through clearly for the first time (and the long E in the bass clarifies the subject's metric shape—bars 1 and 3 weak, 2 and 4 strong—also for the first time).

All this is valedictory, yet the subject now scales heights it never risked before. The soprano reaches up to high B. How will it climb down?

With the greatest of dignity and calm. With no harmonic undercutting and no tumble of faster notes, as in section 1 of the fugue. The harmony under the peak note B is tonic harmony blurred by a suspended A♯ in the tenor—an incredible sound: acquiescent, sheltered, pacific—and this A♯, as it resolves to G♯, seems to draw the upper voice down with it. The soprano response feels like a slow, deep bow . . . touched with something like regret, though feelings are blurred by another suspended note, D♯ in the bass. Even as the fugue quietly gives up aspirations for the heights, it moots confident new possibilities, even now, for breadth. The ritual of measured half notes in the subject builds up from the original seven notes to eight.

The evocation of binary structuring that Bach makes so much of in the Fugue in B-flat Major fades in B Major into a mere suggestion, but an unmistakable suggestion, when the slow trill figure from the end of section 1 is heard again in the soprano, sustained by the tenor *[bars 98–99]*. The counterpoint begins to coalesce into chords, until the second subject returns for the last time, not in its role as a wellspring of counterpoint, but as harmony: a single diminished-seventh chord spreads out under the fingers of both hands, a keyboard player's loose arpeggiation *[bars 100–101]*. To me this is an utterly poignant moment, though like so much else in this work, the poignancy is restrained. The last two bars are pure grace.

It was Riemann's insight that a "turning point" occurs in the fugue after the cadence in bar 60, a turning away from counterpoint toward melody—toward melody and harmony. The turn can be followed bar by bar in the fugue's coda, in bars 97–109.

Of course this is a relative matter; counterpoint is always present. But whereas at first we hear the fugue flex contrapuntal muscle to engage the subject with one countersubject after another, later—after the breach imposed by the long episode—countersubjects are either absent (entry 12), obscured by voice crossing (entry 13), or simply subsidiary, hemmed in by very strong outer voices (entry 14). In the long episode, the soprano pulls away from the lower voices and sings its own song; the cantilena of its whole notes and the bravura of its dotted rhythms are both new to the fugue and expansive. For all the choice details of voice-leading in entry 12, it is the free melodic sequence D♯   C♯ I B . . . ∫ G♯   G♯ F♯ E I D♯ in the soprano that moves us, I think, a melodic shape that is also half-new, a benediction from without (see example 22). To this melody the subject itself becomes a compliant bass.

Stunning moments in this fugue are the outcome of harmonic thinking—bars 75–78, 94–95—and harmony controls more humble passages too, such as the trio-style episode. Friends of this writer will be invited to remember him while listening to this piece, along with the great tranquil Prelude in B-flat Major that belongs with another fugue, the one examined in the previous chapter. The Fugue in B Major will be transposed in honor of its new prelude, even as the moonlighting prelude will hallow its new fugue.